God's Mysterious Ways Revealed

Experiencing Abundant Life in Jesus Christ

By
Frank R. Davis

The oil painting used on the cover entitled, "Third Day of Chanukah" © was painted by Isaac Rivkin. His paintings may be obtained from The Blue and White Art Gallery in Jerusalem. Website: http://www.blueandwhiteart.com

Order this book online at www.trafford.com
or email orders@trafford.com

Most Trafford titles are also available at major online book retailers.

Printed in the United States of America.

ISBN: 978-1-4269-8224-8 (sc)
ISBN: 978-1-4269-8225-5 (e)

Library of Congress Control Number: 2011913323

Trafford rev. 04/27/2012

 www.trafford.com

North America & international
toll-free: 1 888 232 4444 (USA & Canada)
phone: 250 383 6864 ♦ fax: 812 355 4082

ENDORSEMENT FOR "GOD'S MYSTERIOUS WAYS REVEALED"

I have rewritten this foreword several times and each effort falls short of expressing the impact this book will have on anyone who reads it with a hunger to comprehend the mysteries of God's love to bring perfection into the lives of His ultimate creation, man.

"God's Mysterious Ways Revealed" brings us face to face with the necessity of seeing all the events in our lives from the perspective of God's Word.

This book will help you grasp the reality that God's ways are perfect. He is a loving and faithful Father who pursues us with intense actions that are often mistaken for either His anger or His abandonment. Instead of catching a glimpse of God's mercies, His discipline is often falsely identified as His wrath. Nothing could be further from the truth.

Pastor Frank Davis approaches the realities of God's relationship to man gleaned from a life of witnessing God's transforming work in the lives of countless individuals. This book is a balanced in-depth and scriptural study of God's faithfulness to restore His creation to fellowship with Him.

True satisfaction and fulfillment comes from unraveling the mysteries of God's plan to His children who seek hard after Him. "God's Mysterious Ways Revealed" is a scripture based seekers guide into the deep riches of God. If we seek Him with all our heart, we will find Him.

This book is the fruit of years of experience, a shepherd's heart, and a perspective of caring for the flock of God. This book is a rich and valuable tool to unlock God's ways of perfecting men. May each of us be graced to receive the spiritual insights of Pastor Frank's book to interpret and build on the experiences of our lives from God's holy Word.

WITH APPRECIATION FOR A JOB WELL DONE, and a WORD WELL SPOKEN.
Ed Smelser, USA Regional Director
Bridges for Peace, Jerusalem, ISRAEL
www.bridgesforpeace.com

* * * * * * * * * *

"I have known Frank Davis for many years and we've had the privilege of serving the same church at different times. He is committed to Christ and further committed to helping people grow deeper in Christ, and in "God's Mysterious Ways Revealed", Frank helps us do just that. His in-depth focus on scripture will enrich the reader and his insights from experience will add knowledge in a practical way. This book will help those who read it."

Donald E. Ross, Lead Pastor
Creekside Church
7011 226th Pl. SW
PO Box 568
Mountlake Terrace, WA 98043
Ph: 425-778-4165
Fax: 425-778-4837

TABLE OF CONTENTS

INTRODUCTION

The testimony of Katie Souza is just one of literally millions of individuals who have experienced the dealings of God in order to set them free from a destructive self-centered lifestyle. Here is her account of God's dealing in her life as told to Robert Hull of the *700 Club*.

Katie Souza: God's Love Found in Lockdown
By Robert Hull
The 700 Club

http://www.expectedendministries.com
CBN.com – Katie Souza wanted the good life.

"I had all these pre-conceived ideas about what the good life was," Katie Souza tells *The 700 Club*. "I thought if I was working in the entertainment industry that that's the good life. If I've got money, that's the good life. If I'm famous, that's the good life."

Katie pursued her dreams. She says, "I loved radio, because I loved music so much. I thought radio would be really fun, so I got into radio when I was really young. Like 17 years old, I was on the air. I got a job at CBS television, started doing camera work there and doing audio. I was having a lot of fun."

Acting and modeling opportunities followed, but drug use that began in her teens was a full-fledged addiction that threatened everything.

"I was doing all these great things on one hand," she recalls. "I was still empty and horrible even though I had this great thing happening to me. I didn't even know why I was filling myself up with drugs and doing all these things to try to make myself feel satisfied."

Katie was chosen for a role with Universal Studios, but just before her callback, she went on a drug binge.

"I go into this meeting wasted. This guy at Universal looks at me and says, 'You look like a heroin addict. Get out of my office right now.' That was like my last blow. I had gone through all these opportunities, and I'd blown them all. So, I fell face first into crime, and I became a full-time seller. I was already selling to everybody, and then I started cooking meth and collecting."

She was arrested 12 times in one year for multiple felonies. Finally, she was arrested on federal charges for conspiracy, manufacturing narcotics and weapons violations. She was sentenced to 13 years in prison.

"I'm fighting with the cops. I attacked an officer. I'm getting shook down every day in the facility, because I am just starting up problems with all the officers and other inmates there," she explains. "I got thrown in the hole over and over and over again while I'm there."

Finally after a year of violent behavior behind bars, Katie reached her breaking point.

"I had been taken to this lockdown cell that wasn't like a regular lockdown cell. You didn't get a mattress. It's freezing cold. It's covered with urine, vomit and feces. Right then, I got a revelation: 'This is God's way of dealing with you. It took this level of lockdown to get you to break. I'm the only one that can save you out of this.'

"I remember slumping back against that cold cement wall, thinking, 'I can't do this anymore.' I had been fighting everybody out on the streets, and now I'm fighting everybody inside. I didn't even realize I was fighting God Himself. Right then, the Lord spoke to me. 'I want you to surrender to your captivity, because this is My plan and it's perfect.'"

Katie prayed to become a Christian. She read the Bible and shared what she was learning with her fellow inmates.

"The only book in the whole place was the Bible. I remember picking it up, reading through it and I just thought that this is the coolest thing I've ever read in my life. This is amazing. I would go from the front to the back over and over again. As I did that, the Holy Spirit began to point out these Scriptures about these people called the ancient Israelites who went to prison. I was going, 'Wow, this is my story. It's the story of every con I'd ever known. I started getting excited about it, and I started teaching it to everyone that I could teach it to."

Her tough girl attitude and reputation began to change.

"The cops called our unit the 'God Pod,' because everybody's worshipping God. We're baptizing people in the shower. We're praying. There's fellowship going, and this amazing breakout of the presence of God is happening right in the middle of this captivity."

After serving five years of her thirteen-year sentence, Katie won her appeal and was released early. She's free now, and her view of the good life has changed dramatically.

"The good life is having your purpose and having your relationship with God," Katie declares. "There's been so many amazing things that have happened to me since I got out of prison. I quickly discovered that I didn't want to do drugs anymore. I'm so filled up with this relationship with God that I had no desire to do drugs."

Katie wrote a book about the lessons she learned from the Israelites' time in captivity and how God can use prison time to prepare people for their purpose.

"He has a bigger plan an amazing plan where He wants to use captivity to totally give us our dreams, to give us our future. He loves us so much that He's got a plan for it, and it's way bigger than we thought it would be."

The opportunity for meaningful spiritual growth comes to us all in much the same way. God's dealing in our life is never intended to defeat us, but rather to save us and help us gain a heavenly and eternal perspective.

Ephesians 2:2-8 – *"You used to live in sin, just like the rest of the world, obeying the devil—the commander of the powers in the unseen world. He is the spirit at work in the hearts of those who refuse to obey God. All of us used to live that way, following the passionate desires and inclinations of our sinful nature. By our very nature we were subject to God's anger, just like everyone else. But God is so rich in mercy, and he loved us so much, that even though we were dead because of our sins, he gave us life when he raised Christ from the dead. (It is only by God's grace that you have been saved!)*

For he raised us from the dead along with Christ and seated us with him in the heavenly realms because we are united with Christ Jesus. So God can point to us in all future ages as examples of the incredible wealth of his grace and kindness toward us, as shown in all he has done for us who are united with Christ Jesus. God saved you by his grace when you believed. And you can't take credit for this; it is a gift from God." (NLT)

As believers, we have been raised up and seated with Christ in heavenly places. It is a position and placement of intimacy and authority at the Father's right hand. So, God expects us to learn what it means to see life and circumstances from this lofty perspective.

Experiencing God's divine intervention in his life, King David was graced to receive enough spiritual insight so he could interpret the experiences of his life from God's perspective.

<u>**Psa. 119:67, 71-72**</u> – *"Before I was **afflicted** I went astray, but now I obey your word. It was good for me to be afflicted so that I might learn your decrees. The law from your mouth is more precious to me than thousands of pieces of silver and gold."* (NIV)

What an amazingly powerful scripture! David is telling us that "before" he was afflicted by God and the circumstances of life pressed against him, he didn't value God's word like he should; but now having been humbled by God's discipline and chastisement, God's word is more precious than all the wealth this world could ever offer.

Before God steps into our life to correct it, we walk a path that leads to destruction. In fact, until we experience the circumcision of our hearts, we will continually avoid God's right path by looking for the exits and taking various detours. Like sheep, we wander off and go astray.

If a person has been a disciple of Christ for any length of time and has prayerfully desired to be conformed into Christ's glorious image, then, like King David of old, that person has experienced the discipline of God. In fact, if we haven't experienced God's disciplinary action in our lives, we are considered illegitimate children, and not true sons.

<u>**Hebrews 12:7-11**</u> – *"Endure hardship as discipline; God is treating you as sons. For what son is not disciplined by his father? If you are not disciplined (and everyone undergoes discipline), then you are illegitimate children and*

not true sons. Moreover, we have all had human fathers who disciplined us and we respected them for it. How much more should we submit to the Father of our spirits and live! Our fathers disciplined us for a little while as they thought best; but God disciplines us for our good, that we may share in his holiness. No discipline seems pleasant at the time, but painful. Later on, however, it produces a harvest of righteousness and peace for those who have been trained by it." (NIV)

I don't know of anyone who initially relishes chastisement or enjoys correction. However, the man or woman who desires to draw closer to God learns to embrace and accept it.

Among the 3,000 or so proverbs written by Solomon he tells us that a wise man accepts correction and reproof because he knows it's the way of life. Only a fool sloughs off and puts aside disciplinary action and resists correction. Wise people grasp the significance and purpose of affliction, while fools simply gripe and complain.

The wise person understands that affliction is a positive confirmation of our heavenly Father's care and concern for our ultimate well-being. God's divine intervention in our lives is simply the Father's heart seeking our highest good, which is conformity to the image of Christ!

Understanding God's "ways" enables us to cooperate with our heavenly Father's activity in our lives. Instead of resisting His correction, we learn to quickly embrace His loving discipline, in order to share the very nature of Christ, and become pleasing to the Father.

The fact that God has graciously hidden New Testament truths under the blanket of Old Testament types simply allows us to experience, with wondrous awe, the majesty of His saving purpose in Christ.

My prayer is that this book will stimulate and encourage you in your personal search to understand God's high and holy ways, enabling you to cooperate with God as He speaks His living transforming Word into your heart conforming you to the image of His Son.

CHAPTER ONE

The Importance of Understanding God's Ways

Just as when Jesus came into this world in a manner that was not anticipated nor welcomed by the religious establishment, in like manner his death demonstrated that God does not deal with the problem of sin in a manner fallen sinners could have predicted.

Through the prophets, we see the revelation of God's will and purpose unfolding in an incredibly unpredictable fashion. In fact, everything about God's redemptive plan from creation to consummation defies the laws of human logic and reason.

Isaiah 55:8-9 – *"'My thoughts are completely different from yours,' says the Lord. 'And **my ways** are far beyond anything you could imagine. For just as the heavens are higher than the earth, so are **my ways higher than your ways** and my thoughts higher than your thoughts.'"* (NLT)

Deut. 10:12 – *"And now, Israel, what does the Lord your God require from you, but to fear the Lord your God, to **walk in all His ways** and love Him, and to serve the Lord your God with all your heart and with all your soul."* (NASB)

God gave a wonderful promise to Abraham:

Genesis 15:4-5 – *"Then the Lord said to him, 'No, your servant will not be your heir, for you will have a son of your own to inherit everything I am giving you.' Then the Lord brought Abram outside beneath the night* *sky and told him, 'Look up into the heavens and count the stars if you can. Your descendants will be like that—too many to count!' "* (NLT)

But because Abraham and Sarah didn't understand God's ways, they couldn't comprehend why God would make them wait for another 15 years until their bodies were completely incapable of producing children.

Only then, by his resurrection power, did God restore their bodies ability to produce a child and give them Isaac.

However, prior to God's appointed time, Sarah rationalized that God must want Abraham to have a child by Hagar, Sarah's handmaid; and the fact that Abraham listened to Sarah's human reasoning, resulted in the age-old conflict between the descendents of Ishmael (Arabs) and the descendents of Isaac (Jews).

Likewise, our lack of understanding concerning God's ways can also bring devastating consequences into our lives.

In faithfulness, God repeatedly spoke to the spiritual leaders of Israel giving them adequate warning concerning the consequences of failing to obey His law word.

Deut. 30:15-20 – *"Look, today I offer you life and success, death and destruction. I command you today to love the Lord your God, to do what he wants you to do, and to keep his commands, his rules, and his laws. Then you will live and grow in number, and the Lord your God will bless you in the land you are entering to take as your own. But if you turn away from the Lord and do not obey him, if you are led to bow and serve other gods, I tell you today that you will surely be destroyed. And you will not live long in the land you are crossing the Jordan River to enter and take as your own. Today I ask heaven and earth to be witnesses. I am offering you life or death, blessings or curses. Now, choose life! Then you and your children may live. To choose life is to love the Lord your God, obey him, and stay close to him. He is your life, and he will let you live many years in the land, the land he promised to give your ancestors Abraham, Isaac, and Jacob."* (NCV)

Staying close to God and coming to know Him was the path to experiencing the blessings of God. From the time of this warning from Moses, the Old

Testament prophets linked the negative consequences coming upon Israel to their lack of knowing God and understanding His ways.

The prophets of the Old Testament had simply to observe the consequences of Israel's sinful behavior, to understand that ignoring God's word, as well as the revelation of His character and nature, would automatically put the nation of Israel at risk of God's judgment.

Hosea 4:6 – *"My people are being destroyed because they don't know me. Since you priests refuse to know me, I refuse to recognize you as my priests. Since you have forgotten the laws of your God, I will forget to bless your children."* (NLT)

Isaiah 5:13 – *"Therefore my people are gone into captivity, because they have no knowledge: and their honorable men are famished, and their multitude dried up with thirst."* (KJV)

Even in the New Testament, the apostle Paul clearly states in his letters to the Roman Christians and the believers at Ephesus that spiritual captivity and bondage to sin are the realities of not knowing Christ. It is in our coming to know Jesus Christ better that freedom is experienced.

Romans 10:1-3 – *"Dear brothers and sisters, the longing of my heart and my prayer to God is for the people of Israel to be saved. I know what enthusiasm they have for God, but it is misdirected zeal. For they don't understand God's way of making people right with himself. Refusing to accept God's way, they cling to their own way of getting right with God by trying to keep the law."* (NLT)

Eph. 4:17-24 – *"Now this I say and testify in the Lord, that you must no longer walk as the Gentiles do, in the futility of their minds. They are darkened in their understanding, alienated from the life of God because of the ignorance that is in them, due to their hardness of heart.*

They have become callous and have given themselves up to sensuality, greedy to practice every kind of impurity. But you have not so learned Christ, if indeed you have heard Him and have been taught by Him, as the truth is in Jesus: that you put off, concerning your former conduct, the old man which grows corrupt according to the deceitful lusts, and be renewed in the spirit of your mind, and that you put on the new man which was created according to God, in true righteousness and holiness." (NKJV)

Even after coming to Christ and experiencing the regeneration of our human spirit, we are ignorant of His fullness and thus in need of knowing Christ better. In fact, it is only as we come to know Christ that we receive the grace to put off our former manner of life with its corrupt and deceitful desires. The apostle Paul tells us of his personal experience in his letter to the Philippians in chapter 3 and then instructs us on how to put off the old and put on Christ in his letter to the Romans.

Phil. 3:7-11 – *"But Christ has shown me that what I once thought was valuable is worthless. Nothing is as wonderful as knowing Christ Jesus my Lord. I have given up everything else and count it all as garbage. All I want is Christ and to know that I belong to him. I could not make myself acceptable to God by obeying the Law of Moses. God accepted me simply because of my faith in Christ. All I want is to know Christ and the power that raised him to life. I want to suffer and die as he did, so that somehow I also may be raised to life."* (CEV)

Rom. 12:1-2 – *"And so, dear brothers and sisters, I plead with you to give your bodies to God because of all he has done for you. Let them be a living and holy sacrifice—the kind he will find acceptable. This is truly the way to worship him. Don't copy the behavior and customs of this world, but let God transform you into a new person by changing the way you think. Then you will learn to know God's will for you, which is good and pleasing and perfect."* (NLT)

1 Samuel chapters 1-7

This portion of Scripture in the book of Samuel teaches us of God's amazing love and commitment to deliver us from the bondage and domination of the sin nature we all received from Adam. It also instructs us on how to overcome the intrusions of Satan's influence into our lives.

In Romans chapter six the apostle Paul asks the question: "Shall we continue in sin that grace may abound?" And the answer Paul gives us is "God forbid" or "may it never be." It is never God's intention for us to continue in a sinful lifestyle; rather He wants us to experience newness of life and freedom from sin through Christ.

The term "Sin" identifies the fallen Adamic nature that prompts the overt acts (sins), which are a transgression of His law-word: behaviors that are contrary to His holy character and the new nature Christ has given us.

It is not part of God's plan to bless us with the regeneration of our spirit and then leave us in a state of bondage to the dictates of our Adamic sin nature. His plan for us is to experience a glorious freedom to do His will through the strength that Christ provides.

What we need to keep in mind in looking at these seven chapters in 1 Samuel is that there is one overall theme: Understanding God's Ways. Once we gain a greater understanding of His ways, we cease to resist our Father's intervention in our lives and we begin to cooperate with the Holy Spirit by submitting to the truth He speaks into our hearts.

In addition to the overall theme of Understanding God's Ways, we will observe additional lessons and insights related to God's saving activity. Seeing and understanding these spiritual lessons taught in the Old Testament serves to confirm in our hearts the truths taught by the Apostles in the New Testament.

By reviewing numerous Scriptural references we can gain a biblical perspective on the importance of knowing and honoring God's high and holy ways.

Deut. 10:12 – *"And now, Israel, what does the Lord your God require from you, but to fear the Lord your God, to **walk in all His ways** and love Him, and to serve the Lord your God with all your heart and with all your soul."* (NASB)

Deut. 32:4 – *"He is the Rock, his works are perfect, and **all his ways are just**. A faithful God who does no wrong, upright and just is he."* (NIV)

Psa. 18:30 – *"As for God, **his way is perfect**."* (KJV)

Psa. 145:17 – *"The Lord is **righteous in all his ways** and kind in all his works."* (ESV)

Daniel 4:37 – *"Now I, Nebuchadnezzar, praise and extol and honor the King of heaven, for all his works are right and **his ways are just**; and those who walk in pride he is able to humble."* (ESV)

Psalm 103:7 – *"He **made known his ways** to Moses, his deeds to the people of Israel."* (NIV)

Rom. 11:33 – *"Oh, the depth of the riches both of the wisdom and knowledge of God! How unsearchable are His judgments and **His ways** past finding out!"* (NKJV)

Rev. 15:3 – *"**Just and true are your ways**, O King of the nations!"* (ESV)

Isaiah 55:8-9 – *"'My thoughts are completely different from yours,' says the Lord. 'And **my ways** are far beyond anything you could imagine. For just as the heavens are higher than the earth, so are **my ways higher than your ways** and my thoughts higher than your thoughts.'"* (NLT)

2 Chron. 17:6 – *"He was **committed to the ways of the Lord**. He knocked down the pagan shrines and destroyed the Asherah poles."* (NLT)

From the beginning, God has chosen men like Abraham and David who would walk in His ways.

Gen. 18:19 – *"I have singled him out so that he will direct his sons and their families to keep **the way of the Lord** by doing what is right and just. Then I will do for Abraham all that I have promised."* (NLT)

2 Sam 22:22 – *"For I have kept **the ways of the Lord**; I have not turned from my God to follow evil."* (NLT)

2 Chron. 17:6 – *"His heart was devoted to **the ways of the Lord**; furthermore, he removed the high places and the Asherah poles from Judah."* (NIV)

What happens when we walk in **our ways**, instead of walking in **God's ways**?

2 kings 21:22 – *"He forsook the Lord, the God of his fathers, and did not walk in **the way of the Lord**."* (NIV)

Deut. 28:28-29 – *"The Lord will strike you with madness and blindness and confusion of heart. And you shall grope at noonday, as a blind man gropes in darkness; **you shall not prosper in your ways**; you shall be only oppressed and plundered continually, and no one shall save you."* (NKJV)

Judges 2:22 – *"I will no longer drive out before them any of the nations Joshua left when he died. I will use them to test Israel and see whether they will keep **the way of the Lord** and walk in it as their forefathers did."* (NIV)

When Joshua failed to conquer all the inhabitants of Canaan, the Lord purposed to use those tribes to test the Israelites' commitment to walk in His ways. Then in Jeremiah's day, the majority of Israelites chose to conform to the societies around them and refused to walk in the way of the Lord.

Jer. 5:3-6 – *"Lord, don't you look for truth in people? You struck the people of Judah, but they didn't feel any pain. You crushed them, but they refused to learn what is right. They became more stubborn than a rock; they refused to turn back to God. But I thought, 'These are only the poor, foolish people. They have not learned **the way of the Lord** and what their God wants them to do. So I will go to the leaders of Judah and talk to them. Surely they understand **the way of the Lord** and know what God wants them to do.' But even the leaders had all joined together to break away from the Lord; they had broken their ties with him. So a lion from the forest will attack them. A wolf from the desert will kill them. A leopard is waiting for them near their towns. It will tear to pieces anyone who comes out of the city, because the people of Judah have sinned greatly. They have wandered away from the Lord many times."* (CEV)

Jer. 6:16 – *"So now the LORD says, 'Stop right where you are! Look for the old, **godly way**, and walk in it. Travel its path, and you will find rest for your souls.' But you reply, 'No, that's not the road we want!' "* (NLT)

Hosea 14:9 – *"If you are wise, you will know and understand what I mean. I am the LORD, and I lead you along **the right path**. If you obey me, we will walk together, but if you are wicked, you will stumble."* (CEV)

When you look at the resulting consequences of failing to walk in God's ways, you can understand why Moses and the Psalmist prayed:

Ex. 33:13 – *"Now therefore, if I have found favor in your sight, please **show me now your ways, that I may know you** in order to find favor in your sight."*

Psalm 25:4 – *"Show me **your ways**, O Lord, teach me **your** paths."* (NIV)

Isaiah 2:3 – *"Many nations will come and say, 'Come, let us go up to the mountain of the Lord, to the Temple of the God of Israel. There **he will teach us his ways, so that we may obey him**.'"* (NLT)

Prior to his conversion, the apostle Paul had great zeal, but not according to knowledge and so he persecuted any who were trying to follow Jesus.

Acts 22:4 – *"I persecuted the people who followed **the Way of Jesus**, and some of them were even killed. I arrested men and women and put them in jail."* (CEV)

However, once he encountered the risen Christ, his testimony changed completely.

Acts 24:14 – *"But I will tell you this: I worship the God of our ancestors **as a follower of the Way of Jesus**. The others say that the Way of Jesus is not the right way. But I believe everything that is taught in the law of Moses and that is written in the books of the Prophets."* (CEV)

Psa. 138:5 – *"Yes, they will sing about **the Lord's ways**, for the glory of the Lord is very great."* (NLT)

The consistent weekly gathering of the Church of Jesus Christ is an opportunity we may all take advantage of to come before His presence and seek to be taught of the Lord, learning His ways, so that we can obey Him.

Our success in obeying the Lord and walking in His ways is directly related to our ability to draw upon the life of Christ living within us, and that ability is only realized when we are delivered from trusting in our own ways.

It was following my surrender to the Lordship of Christ and subsequent baptism in the Holy Spirit, when I began to exercise my faith by praying for individuals who were sick, believing that God still heals today; and God has graciously allowed me to witness numerous miraculous healings.

While attending Northwest College, I had the opportunity of traveling to Guyana, South America on a summer mission's internship with Paul Wheeler, a fellow student. God demonstrated His saving grace and power allowing me to witness many individuals coming to a saving knowledge of Jesus, and also observing Jesus healing the sick, delivering the demon possessed, and baptizing many young people in the Holy Spirit.

I had the privilege of prayerfully asking Jesus to heal a 10-year-old boy who was totally deaf, and then, I experienced the excitement of rejoicing with his family and friends as he began to speak and respond to what he was hearing.

It was following that summer internship in Guyana, South America and while still attending Northwest College that God began to deal with me about the importance of knowing Him and understanding His ways. My return to the new school year was filled with excitement and great anticipation of what God might do in my life and in the lives of my fellow students.

At the beginning of the new school year, Paul and I shared about our summer experiences in a special chapel service and then took time to pray for any students who wanted a fresh touch from the Lord.

The Lord graciously touched many students, some were healed, and others were released in faith to function in the gifts of the Spirit, and a few received visions from the Lord.

Following these wonderful experiences in Christ, I imagined myself being involved in "turning the world upside down" for Jesus. Although several students were touched by Christ and healed as we prayed for them, what followed was not what I expected. What followed was a period of spiritual barrenness.

In His glorious wisdom, God simply withdrew the conscious awareness of His presence from my life. Prior to this experience of emptiness, I could always drop to my knees and call upon the name of the Lord and confidently feel His holy presence. Suddenly, things were different.

Determined not to allow the enemy to take my joy from all the wonderful things that God had wrought throughout the previous summer, I took time to fast and pray, seeking the Lord and resisting the enemy. But the emptiness continued.

In desperation I cried out to the Lord, asking Him to reveal my sin or whatever it was blocking my communion with Him and sense of His presence… no answer. I then told the Lord it was no use for me to continue preparing for fulltime pastoral ministry if I couldn't receive input from Him and experience His holy presence.

Finally, the day of divine encounter occurred as I knelt at my bed. Suddenly, the presence of God enveloped me and I began to weep uncontrollably.

After a couple of minutes, the Lord spoke to me and said simply, "You know the work of My hands, but you don't know Me."

While He was speaking those words, all the miraculous happenings of the past three years flashed before my eyes and in brokenness I responded, "Lord, even if I never see another miracle, I want to know You."

That experience launched me on a most exciting adventure of learning what it means to know the Lord and understand His ways. The Holy Spirit instructed me to begin praying a prayer based on Paul's prayer for the Ephesian church:

Eph. 1:17-19 – *"I keep asking that the God of our Lord Jesus Christ, the glorious Father, may give you (me) the Spirit of wisdom and revelation, so that (I) you may know him better. I pray also that the eyes of (my) your heart may be enlightened in order that (I) you may know the hope to which he has called (me) you, the riches of his glorious inheritance in the saints, and his incomparably great power for us who believe. That power is like the working of his mighty strength."* (NIV)

What a tremendous blessing has resulted in my life!

My prayer for you is that as you read this book, you too will embrace a pursuit of seeking to know God more intimately and come to understand His ways more completely. Oh, that we may obey Him completely.

In the next chapter we will endeavor to understand the saving work of God more fully. By examining the Scriptures, we come to understand that our salvation in Christ is both "positional" and "experiential."

CHAPTER TWO

The Process of God's Saving Grace

How is it that people who identify themselves as Christians can claim to be "saved", and yet still gossip about fellow Christians, still tell lies, still take things that don't belong to them, become involved in immoral relationships, and still think they are saved? How can they explode with anger and revenge against a neighbor's despiteful behavior when the Lord Jesus commanded, "Love your neighbor as yourself" and "Do good to those who mistreat you?"

In answering these questions, it is imperative for you to recognize that salvation for the believer in Christ is a **past**, **present**, and **future** experience. What do I mean?

As I said before, salvation is **past** (in that we **have been** regenerated in our human spirit, which was dead in trespasses and sins), it is **present** (in that we **are being** saved in our soul), and it is **future** (in that we **will receive** our resurrection body at the resurrection of the righteous, receiving a body just like the Lord's body). (Eph. 2:1)(Heb. 10:39)(1 Cor. 15:42-57)(KJV)

God's original intention of conforming us to the image of Christ can only be accomplished as we become sharers and partakers of His divine nature (Rom. 8:29)(2 Peter 1:2-4).

In order to accomplish this glorious purpose God must redeem us from "the wages of sin," which is spiritual and physical death, and in addition, He must also deliver us from our "bondage to sin", as expressed in sinful attitudes and behavior.

The Lord does this by, first of all, giving us a new nature, the very life and nature of Christ, and then He teaches us how to draw upon that life, which is resident in our spirit, so that we can live victoriously as Christians. Jesus put it in simple terms when he said, *"You must be born again."*

When we open our heart to the truth that Jesus is the Lamb of God who takes away the sins of the world and by faith repent of our sinful independence from God and receive Jesus into our lives as Lord and Savior, the Scripture assures us that we are born again. The Holy Spirit then bears witness with our spirit that we are now a child of God; however, at that moment, we are ignorant of what really happens internally when we believe on the Lord Jesus Christ, placing our trust in His saving grace and atoning work on the cross.

So, what actually happens when we are "born again?"

Before I share with you the Scriptures that answer that question, we need to understand the additional truth of how God created us.

I. How God Created Us.

1 Thess. 5:23 – *"I pray that God, who gives peace, will make you completely holy. And may your **spirit**, **soul**, and **body** be kept healthy and faultless until our Lord Jesus Christ returns."* (CEV)

God made us a tripartite being – spirit, soul, and body. Our **spirit** makes us God-conscious. Our **soul**, comprising our mind, will, and emotions, makes us self-conscious and our **body** with its five senses (taste, touch, smell, sight, and hearing) makes us world-conscious. (For a more in-depth study of spirit, soul, and body, I recommend Watchman Nee's book entitled *The Spiritual Man*).

God's temporary house that enabled Him to dwell with man in the Old Testament was the Tabernacle. The Tabernacle consisted of three parts: the Most Holy Place (the residence of God's presence), the Holy Place, and the Outer Court. Each of the parts of the Tabernacle corresponds to the three parts of man. In other words, the **temporary** dwelling place of God (the Tabernacle) resembles God's **permanent** dwelling place (man).

1 Cor. 3:16-17 – *"Don't you realize that all of you together are the temple of God and that the Spirit of God lives in you? If anyone destroys God's temple, God will destroy that person, because God's temple is holy and you are that temple."*

1 Cor. 6:19-20 – *"Don't you realize that your body is the temple of the Holy Spirit, who lives in you and was given to you by God? You do not belong to yourself, for God bought you with a high price. So you must honor God with your body."*

Understanding that the pattern of the Old Testament Tabernacle is a picture of the New Testament eternal house God desires, we can then understand that as God's eternal house we have been set apart as His holy dwelling place.

We are a three-fold being: **spirit** (where God's Spirit dwells and communion takes place), **soul** (where sanctification is taking place as we gain the mind of Christ, express the fruits of the Holy Spirit, and obediently learn how to worship in spirit and truth) and **body** (through which we demonstrate the will of God in word and deed).

II. How God Saves Us.

When God created this world and everything in it, He made everything "good" and never purposed for us to suffer sickness, death, war, and heartache. Those life experiences are the results of Adam's choice to reject and disobey the living word of God.

What God is presently doing through Christ (the eternal Word) is reaching down into our dark pit of bondage and slavery to the rebellious nature of sin and rescuing us out of that pit, giving us a new nature through the regeneration of our human spirit, and thus restoring us into fellowship with Him.

By rejecting God's prohibition against eating from the tree of the knowledge of good and evil, Adam, the head of the old creation, sinned and the nature of sin was passed to the entire human race (Romans 5:12-14). In this sinful condition, all of mankind was separated from God's holy presence and intimate fellowship with Him.

We know from Scripture that, through the work of Christ on the cross, the veil separating the Holy Place from the Most Holy Place was torn from top to bottom indicating two wonderful truths: **first**, that through Christ's atoning work on Calvary, God has given all New Testament believer-priests access to His Holy presence; and **second**, that God's redemptive work through Christ enables Him to fill His entire dwelling place (our spirit, soul, and body) with the glory of His presence.

Heb. 4:16 – *"So let us come boldly to the throne of our gracious God. There we will receive his mercy, and we will find grace to help us when we need it most."*

So, what happens when we are born again?

Eph. 2:1-10 – *"In the past you were spiritually dead because of your sins and the things you did against God. Yes, in the past you lived the way the world lives, following the ruler of the evil powers that are above the earth. That same spirit is now working in those who refuse to obey God. In the past all of us lived like them, trying to please our sinful selves and doing all the things our bodies and minds wanted. We should have suffered God's anger because we were sinful by nature. We were the same as all other people. But God's mercy is great, and he loved us very much. Though we were spiritually dead because of the things we did against God, he gave us new life with Christ. You have been saved by God's grace. And he raised us up with Christ and gave us a seat with him in the heavens. He did this for those in Christ Jesus so that for all future time he could show the very great riches of his grace by being kind to us in Christ Jesus. I mean that you have been saved by grace through believing. You did not save yourselves; it was a gift from God."* (NCV)

Paul's letter to the Ephesian believers points out that they were "spiritually dead." Dead does not mean our human spirit is "non-existent;" rather it simply indicates the condition of our spirit, which is the "absence of life"; just as a dark room simply indicates the absence of light. That's why Jesus said, *"I am the light of the world. He who follows Me shall not walk in darkness, but have the light of life."* (John 8:12)

Upon believing in Jesus and receiving Christ as our redeemer, the Spirit of Christ, the source of life takes up residence in our human spirit imparting the very life of God. At that point we often declare the "positional" truth that we are "saved."

It is true that "positionally," Christ's suffering in spirit, soul and body on the cross provided a complete redemption for us and we are raised up and seated with Him at the right hand of God Almighty. However, although our spirit has been made alive with the very life of Christ, our soul is still in need of being saved "experientially".

What do I mean? Well, just as the Holy Place in the Tabernacle contains three pieces of furniture, the Candelabra, the Altar of Incense, and the Table of Showbread, the soul consists of three corresponding parts: mind, will, and emotions.

When Jesus came into the world, his testimony was: *"I'm here to do it your way, O God, the way it's described in your Book."* <u>Heb. 10:7</u> (Msg)

1 John 2:6 – *"He who says he abides in Him ought himself also to walk just as He walked."* (NKJV)

Paul tells us that in order to have the mind of Christ and demonstrate His life before the world; we must experience a transformation in the way we think. Our minds must be renewed. Our will must become submitted to the will of God in all things, following Jesus' example; and our emotions must express the fruit of the Holy Spirit.

Rom. 12:2 – *"Do not conform any longer to the pattern of this world, but be transformed by the renewing of your mind. Then you will be able to test and approve what God's will is—his good, pleasing and perfect will."* (NIV)

Eph. 5:17 – *"Therefore do not be foolish, but understand what the will of the Lord is."* (ESV)

Gal. 5:16, 22-25 – *"So I say, let the Holy Spirit guide your lives. Then you won't be doing what your sinful nature craves. But the Holy Spirit produces this kind of fruit in our lives: love, joy, peace, patience, kindness, goodness, faithfulness, gentleness, and self-control. There is no law against these things! Those who belong to Christ Jesus have nailed the passions and desires of their sinful nature to his cross and crucified them there. Since* *we are living by the Spirit, let us follow the Spirit's leading in every part of our lives."*

So, as I said before, salvation for the believer is **past** (we have been regenerated in our spirit), **present** (experientially, we are being saved in our soul), and **future** (we will receive our resurrection body, just like the Lord's body, at the resurrection of the righteous).

Heb. 10:39 – *"But we are not of those who draw back to perdition, but of those who believe to the saving of the soul."* (NKJV)

1 Pet. 1:8-9 – *"Though you have not seen him, you love him. Though you do not now see him, you believe in him and rejoice with joy that is inexpressible and filled with glory, obtaining the outcome of your faith, the salvation of your souls."* (ESV)

Phil. 2:12 – *"Therefore, my dear friends, as you have always obeyed—not only in my presence, but now much more in my absence—continue to work out your salvation with fear and trembling."* (NIV)

Working out one's salvation has nothing to do with the finished work of Christ, but has everything to do with whether or not we live the Christian life in victory or defeat. Living and walking in victory is directly related to how well we come to know the Lord and understand God's ways.

It is always an agonizing tragedy when the secret sins of a believer are exposed to the entire world.

Jesus said, *"For all that is secret will eventually be brought into the open, and everything that is concealed will be brought to light and made known to all."* (Luke 8:17)

God's way is love. He loves us enough to confront us. He loves us enough to not let us continue in sinful behavior, so He exposes us and brings to light what is hidden so we will acknowledge our sin, repent, and be healed.

In the following illustrations, which describe the trichodomy of man, we can identify the condition of man **after** the Fall, and man's condition **after** experiencing new birth in Christ.

MAN'S SPIRITUAL CONDITION *PRIOR* TO NEW BIRTH IN CHRIST

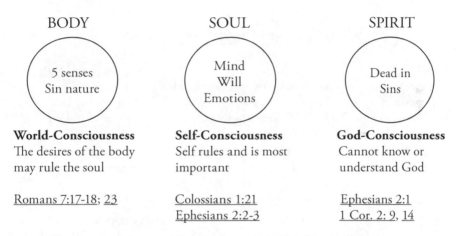

BODY	SOUL	SPIRIT
5 senses Sin nature	Mind Will Emotions	Dead in Sins
World-Consciousness The desires of the body may rule the soul	**Self-Consciousness** Self rules and is most important	**God-Consciousness** Cannot know or understand God
Romans 7:17-18; 23	Colossians 1:21 Ephesians 2:2-3	Ephesians 2:1 1 Cor. 2: 9, 14

Eph. 2:1 – *"Once you were **dead** because of your disobedience and your many sins."*

When Jesus died on the cross, He dealt with our sin problem in two ways. First, by dying on the cross. He paid the penalty for our sins, because "the wages of sin is death." Second, He dealt with the sin nature that prompts the sinful acts that we commit.

When reading the sixth chapter of Romans, it's important to understand that Paul's reference to "sin" is a reference to the sin nature we received from Adam. His reference to "sins" (plural) is a reference to the behavior, in word, attitude, and deed, which the sin nature prompts in us.

MAN'S SPIRITUAL CONDITION *AFTER* NEW BIRTH IN CHRIST

Worldly Knowledge   God's Revelation Knowledge

5 senses
Sin nature

Mind
Will
Emotions

—CHRIST—

World-Consciousness   **Self-Consciousness**   **God-Consciousness**

Galatians 5:16-21	Romans 12:2	Galatians 5:22-25
Sin no longer reigns when our bodily members are yielded to God.	Self becomes less and less important until Christ becomes preeminent.	A person can now know God as He reveals Himself through Jesus Christ.
John 8:31-32	Colossians 1:15-19	1 Corinthians 6:1
Rom. 6:14	Ephesians 4:17-18, 20-25	1 Corinthians 2:10-12

All of our life we have been receiving information through our five senses and cataloging it in our mind and then justifying our self-centered and independent behavior. However, our five senses are all open to deception and the conclusions we draw from the information we receive are subject to the worldview we have received from godless philosophies and ideologies.

But once we receive Christ as Lord and Savior, God, the Holy Spirit, begins to teach us from the Scriptures and speak truth into our human spirit. The truth of God then conflicts with and confronts the worldly knowledge resident in our soul, which we have received from the world-system that dominates most educational institutions as well as the media; and then the battle begins in the mind forcing us to decide if we are going to believe God's Word or the reasoning's of man.

Jesus described his personal struggle with the surrender of his will, as he prepared to go to the cross. Realize – none of us escape this same struggle.

John 12:27 – *"Now my soul is deeply troubled. Should I pray, 'Father, save me from this hour'? But this is the very reason I came!"*

<u>**Luke 22:42**</u> – *"Father, if you are willing, please take this cup of suffering away from me. Yet I want your will to be done, not mine."*

THE BELIEVER'S NEED FOR SOUL TRANSFORMATION AND DELIVERANCE FROM BODILY LUSTS

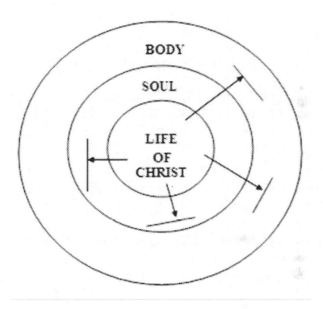

As a new believer, the Spirit of Christ has taken up residence in our human spirit and we are a new creation in Christ Jesus. The problem for every new believer is that our soul and body are not automatically conformed to this new life within. Until the mind is renewed our decisions and choices block the expression of Christ and if our bodily desires rule, they will block the expression of Christ.

In order for the new life of Christ to find expression through our soul, we must have our **mind** renewed by the Word of God, so we can gain the mind of Christ; our **will** must be brought into subjection to God's will, as stated in the Word; and our **emotions** must become yielded to the Holy Spirit, so we can express the fruit of the Spirit instead of manifesting in fleshly emotions.

Therefore, once we have been born again, in order to walk in victory over the sin nature, which dwells in our mortal body, it requires that we clearly **identify** with Christ in His death, burial, and resurrection, through water baptism; and then, in the moment or hour of temptation, we must **reckon** upon the fact that we have already died **with Christ** when He died to sin, and rose **with Him** to walk in newness of life by God's gracious enablement.

Then, we must actively and aggressively **yield** our members as instruments of righteousness unto God in order to avoid the snare of the enemy and avoid manifesting sinful behavior.

Steps to victory in Christ from Romans chapter 6: Know, Reckon, and Yield.

1. **Knowing this (vs. 6):** Rather than merely giving mental assent to the truth, understand by the quickening of the Holy Spirit that when He died, your "old self" with its rebellious nature died with Him.
2. **Reckon upon that fact (vs.11):** Mentally recall your identification with Christ rather than identifying with your Adamic nature.
3. **Actively Yield Your Members (vs. 13):** Turn to God; flee or run for your life from unrighteousness. Bring every thought captive to the obedience of Christ.

Because Jesus provided a full salvation for us, we are given a positional standing of righteousness with Almighty God. However, to experience the benefits of this positional standing we must apply the truth of God's Word in practical daily living.

As redeemed members of the family of God, we now have two natures to deal with and it is vital to understand which nature is prompting our behavior. Which nature are we identifying with on a daily basis? Unless the Word of God has renewed our mind, we will subconsciously revert back to our old ways of doing things, which is not God's way.

Gal. 5:16-26 – *"So I say, let the Holy Spirit guide your lives. Then you won't be doing what your sinful nature craves. The sinful nature wants to do evil, which is just the opposite of what the Spirit wants. And the Spirit gives us desires that are the opposite of what the sinful nature desires. These* *two forces are constantly fighting each other, so you are not free to carry out your good intentions. But when you are directed by the Spirit, you are not under obligation to the law of Moses. When you follow the desires of your sinful nature, the results are very clear: sexual immorality, impurity, lustful pleasures, idolatry, sorcery, hostility, quarreling, jealousy, outbursts of anger, selfish ambition, dissension, division, envy, drunkenness, wild parties, and other sins like these. Let me tell you again, as I have before, that anyone living that sort of life will not inherit the Kingdom of God.*

But the Holy Spirit produces this kind of fruit in our lives: love, joy, peace, patience, kindness, goodness, faithfulness, gentleness, and self-control. There is no law against these things! Those who belong to Christ Jesus have nailed the passions and desires of their sinful nature to his cross and crucified them there. Since we are living by the Spirit, let us follow the Spirit's leading in every part of our lives." (NLT)

Because we are prone to sinful behavior due to our Adamic fallen nature and sinful habit patterns, it often takes a crisis in our lives to expose and make us aware that the sin nature is actually dominating our behavior.

Have you ever heard anyone ask this question: "Why does God allow bad things to happen to good people?"

Throughout human history that question and similar questions have been asked by many thousands of believers, as well as nonbelievers. And because we have not understood God's ways, many have ignorantly embraced erroneous concepts about God and His character when confronted with personal adversity.

Once a person has experienced personal devastation and loss, their ability to once again trust God with their lives can be hindered and the ability to trust God is only regained, when we come to know and believe the truth about God as revealed in Scripture.

His Word declares that God is light and there is no darkness in Him. It says He is Love and seeks only our highest good. Therefore, we must look at adversity from this lofty perspective.

When things are going well, we don't feel we need God. However, when our life starts falling apart, we are driven to the only One who can rescue us and make even bad experiences work for our good. As God works good into our bad situation, we become stronger, grow in our faith and become more like Christ. That's why adversity and often personal loss is one of God's greatest tools for growing us spiritually.

Joni Eareckson Tada, at the age of 17, became paralyzed from the neck down after a diving accident and it changed her life forever. She says:

"One hot July afternoon in 1967, I dove into a shallow lake and my life changed forever. I suffered a spinal cord fracture that left me paralyzed from the neck down, without use of my hands and legs. Lying in my hospital bed, I tried desperately to make sense of the horrible turn of events. I begged friends to assist me in suicide. Slit my wrists, dumped pills down my throat, anything to end my misery!

I had so many questions. **I believed in God, but I was angry with Him.** How could my circumstance be a demonstration of His love and power? Surely He could have stopped it from happening. How can permanent, lifelong paralysis be a part of His loving plan for me? Unless I found answers, I didn't see how this God could be worthy of my trust.

Steve, a friend of mine, took on my questions. He pointed me to Christ. Now I believe that God's purpose in my accident was to turn a stubborn kid into a woman who would reflect patience, endurance and a lively, optimistic hope of the heavenly glories above.[1]

"In the Psalms we're told that God does not deal with us according to our sins and iniquities. My accident was not a punishment for my wrongdoing – whether or not I deserved it. Only God knows why I was paralyzed. Maybe He knew I'd be ultimately happier serving Him. If I were still on my feet, it's hard to say how things may have gone. I probably would have drifted through life – marriage, maybe even divorce – dissatisfied and disillusioned. When I was in high school, I reacted to life selfishly, and almost always at the expense of others, and never built on any long-lasting values." "But now you're happy?" a teen-age girl asked. "I really am. I wouldn't change my life for anything. I feel privileged. God doesn't give such special attention to everyone and intervene that way in their lives. He allows most people to go right on in their own ways. He doesn't interfere even though He knows they are ultimately destroying their own lives, health or happiness, and it must

---

[1]   http://powertochange.com/changed/jeareckson

grieve him terribly. I'm really thankful He did something to get my attention and change me. You know, you don't have to get a broken neck to be drawn to God. But the truth is, people don't always listen to the experiences of others and learn from them. I hope you'll learn from my experience, though, and not have to go through the bitter lessons of suffering which I had to face in order to learn." [2] From "Joni" The Epilogue.

James 1:2-4 – *"Count it all joy, my brothers, when you meet trials of various kinds, for you know that the testing of your faith produces steadfastness. And let steadfastness have its full effect, that you may be perfect and complete, lacking in nothing."* (ESV)

Psa. 12:6 – *"The words and promises of the Lord are pure words, like silver refined in an earthen furnace, purified **seven** times over."* (AMP)

Every word, God speaks into your life and mine, will be tried as silver is refined and purified until that purification process is complete.

Some numbers in biblical usage have symbolic meaning. **Seven** represents completeness and perfection, as seen in the seven days of creation and the corresponding seven-day week, climaxing with the Sabbath (Gen. 1:1-2:4).

In Pharaoh's dream, there were seven good years followed by seven years of famine (Gen. 41:1-36). Jacob worked seven years for Rachel, etc.

A similar use of the number seven can be seen in the NT. There are seven churches mentioned in Revelation 2-3 and seven deacons in Acts 6:1-6. When Peter asked the question about forgiveness, Jesus responded that we are not to forgive just seven times, but seventy times seven (Matt. 18:21-22).

Multiples of seven were also important as illustrated in these passages: Dan. 9:2; Lev. 25:8-55; Exodus 24:1, 9; Jer. 25:12, 29:10; Luke 10:1-17.

Seven is the biblical number of completion, which means that God is committed to work in our lives until the work He started is completed. Thanks be to God!

Phil. 1:6 – *"And I am convinced and sure of this very thing, that He Who began a good work in you will continue until the day of Jesus Christ [right*

---

[2]   http://christianlibrary.org.au/cel/homeschool/joni.html

up to the time of His return], developing [that good work] and perfecting and bringing it to full completion in you." (AMP)

God is refining the church in order to make her pure. When gold is taken from the ground, it contains impurities. In this unrefined state, the gold is hard and cannot be used to make fine jewelry. In the same way, a hardened heart left unrefined remains full of pride, anger, lust, bitterness and self-will. Therefore, the refiner places the gold into the fire in order to separate the impurities from the gold. This is a delicate process so the refiner stays with the gold, carefully watching over it. The fire causes the impurities to rise to the surface and become exposed. Then the impurities are removed from the gold and the pure gold becomes soft and flexible, much like a purified heart becomes soft, tender and pliable and responsive to God's directing.

Jer. 9:7 – *"So this is what the LORD All-Powerful says: 'I will test the people of Judah as a person tests metal in a fire. I have no other choice, because my people have sinned."* (NIV)

God, like the refiner who purifies gold and silver with fire, purifies the church making us holy, blameless and pure. God refines His children in the furnace of suffering.

Why do you and I encounter suffering and hardship at the mercy of the Refiner? Not to be destroyed, but to be recreated in His image. God envisions a kingdom or family of individuals conformed into the image of His Son.

Rom. 8:29 – *"For those whom he foreknew he also predestined to be conformed to the image of his Son, in order that he might be the firstborn among many brothers."* (ESV)

So, He chooses us, while full of sinful impurities, and begins delivering us from the domination of our sin nature and the influences of a dirty, sinful world, with the vision to make us, soft, pure, useable, and Christ-like.

Col. 1:21 – *"This includes you who were once far away from God. You were his enemies, separated from him by your evil thoughts and actions."* (NLT)

Our **human spirit** has been regenerated and made alive by the indwelling of God's Holy Spirit.

Our **soul** is presently being saved as we humbly surrender **our will** to God's will, which is revealed to us in His Holy Word by the Holy Spirit.

The Word of God is renewing **our mind** as we meditate on it day and night, and the Holy Spirit teaches us God's ways.

As we learn to yield **our emotions** to the Holy Spirit, we are learning as well to express His love, joy, peace, patience, kindness, goodness, faithfulness, gentleness, and self-control.

This is victorious Christian living. Living by the life of Christ dwelling within us; the very thing God is desirous for each of us to experience.

There are Christians who mistakenly think that the sin nature is eradicated once you believe on the Lord Jesus Christ. But Scripture clearly teaches us that the war between our sin nature and the Holy Spirit continues right up to the time we put off this mortal body in death.

Therefore, we must allow the Lord to expose:

- the areas in which we are already conformed to this world-system, so our mind can be renewed by God's Word;

- the areas in which our fleshly desires dominate, so we can embrace death to self;

- the areas of our lives in which the enemy has established strongholds, hindering us from living victoriously in Christ, so we can walk in a manner pleasing to the Father.

CHAPTER THREE

The Role of Types in the Scriptures.

Since so little is known about "Typology" among Christians as a whole, I felt it would be important to help each reader get a grasp of its important role in communicating the majesty and wondrous wisdom of God's redemptive plan.

The spiritual lessons God has placed within this specific passage of scripture in 1 Samuel are disclosed to us by the Holy Spirit through the medium of types. Typology is simply the study of types. It is a branch of biblical interpretation in which an element found in the Old Testament prefigures one found in the New Testament.

I. Understanding Typology

"Typology is a way of setting forth the biblical history of salvation so that some of its earlier phases are seen as anticipations of later phases, or some later phase as the recapitulation or fulfillment of an earlier one.

In the language of typology, the earlier series of events constituted a 'type' of the later; the later series was an 'antitype' of the earlier. Or it may be said that the successive epochs of salvation-history disclose a recurring pattern of divine activity, which the NT writers believed to have found its definitive expression in their own day.

The typological relation between the two Testaments was summed up in Augustine's epigram: 'In the OT the NT lies hidden; in the NT the OT stands revealed.' In the NT the Christian salvation is presented as the climax of the mighty works of God, as the 'antitype' of his 'typical' mighty works in the OT. The Christian salvation is treated as a new creation, a new exodus, and a new restoration from exile." [3]

A "type" is a prefigure, as Abraham's offering up Isaac was a prefigure of the sacrifice of Christ.

An example of typology: Isaac as a type of Jesus.

	ISAAC	JESUS
Only begotten Son	Genesis 22:2	John 3:16
Offered on a mountain, hill	22:2	Matt. 21:10
Took donkey to place of sacrifice	22:3	Matt. 21:2–11
Two men went with him.	22:3	Mark 15:27; Luke 23:33
Three-day journey. Jesus: three days in the grave	22:4	Luke 24:13–21
Son carried wood on his back up hill	22:6	John 19:17
God will provide for Himself the lamb	22:8	John 1:29
Son was offered on the wood	22:9	Luke 23:33
Ram in thicket of thorns	22:13	John 19:2
The seed will be multiplied	22:17	John 1:12; Isa. 53:10
Abraham went down, Son didn't, "not mentioned."	22:19	Luke 23:46
Servant gets bride for son	24:1–4	Eph. 5:22–32; Rev. 21:2, 9; 22:17
The bride was a beautiful virgin	24:16	2 Cor. 11:2
Servant offered ten gifts to bride*	24:10	Rom. 6:23; Rom. 12; 1 Cor. 12

---

[3] @book Woo-3467, author = Wood, D. R. W.; Marshall, I. Howard}, title = New Bible Dictionary, publisher = InterVarsity Press, address = Downers Grove, year = 1996, c1982, c1962, pages = 1214, keywords = Bible, edition = electronic ed. of 3rd ed., descriptor = Includes index.

FRANK R. DAVIS

The **prefigure** is called a "type" and the **fulfillment** is designated as the "antitype." Either type or antitype may be a person, thing, or event, but often a biblical type is messianic and frequently references our salvation in Christ. For example:

- **As a person:** In **Romans 5:14** – *"Yet death reigned from Adam to Moses, even over those whose sinning was not like the transgression of Adam, who was a type of the one who was to come. If, because of one man's trespass, death reigned through that one man, much more will those who receive the abundance of grace and the free gift of righteousness reign in life through the one man Jesus Christ."* (NASB)

-

We see that Adam is called a type (Greek - *typos*) of the one who was to come, referring to Christ, the last Adam. Adam is the federal head of the old creation, and Christ is the federal head of the new creation; and as a result, all of humanity is viewed as being either 'in Adam' or 'in Christ'.

Thus, Adam is a type of Christ, and Christ is the antitype of Adam.

Thankfully, by God we have *been "rescued from the kingdom of darkness and transferred into the Kingdom of His dear Son."* (Col. 1:13) (NLT)

Although no other character in the Old Testament is expressly designated as a type (*typos*) of Christ in the New Testament, many other Old Testament characters typify him either by comparison or contrast.

The New Testament teaches that Jonah (Matt. 12:39–41), Adam (Rom. 5:14), Solomon (Matt. 12:42), David (Luke 6:3–4), and Moses (Heb. 3) are all types of Jesus Christ.

Moses compared Christ's prophetic ministry to his own (Acts 3:22). In Hebrews 5 the writer to the Hebrews contrasts Aaron's temporary priestly ministry to the permanent ministry of Christ who was appointed as a priest forever after the order of Melchizedek.

- **As a thing:** Jesus said, *"As Moses lifted up the serpent in the wilderness, so must the Son of Man be lifted up"* (John 3:14). (ESV) In addition, both John the Baptist and the apostle Paul clearly state that Jesus Christ is the antitype of the Passover lamb (John 1:29)(1 Cor. 5:7).

- **As an event:** The apostle Paul clearly compares a believer's regeneration and the experience of newness of life in Christ to the original creation in his letter to the Corinthian believers. 2 Cor. 4:6 – "God once said, 'Let the light shine out of the darkness!' This is the same God who made his light shine in our hearts by letting us know the glory of God that is in the face of Christ." (NCV) In addition, John's gospel makes this same comparison to the event of creation, when he refers to Christ, "In the beginning was the Word...." (John 1:1)

"It is only in the light of the antitype that the relevance of the type can be appreciated." [4]

A type is different from a symbol. Symbols can refer to something past, present, or future, however, a type always foreshadows that which is to come. A type, just as with an illustration or a parable, cannot be pressed in all of its details.

However, there are details, which are singled out as types. For example, in the directions for the celebration of the Feast of Passover, when preparing the lamb for a household, God told the Israelites, *"you shall not break a bone of it"* (Ex. 12:46)(Psa. 34:20)(John 19:31-36).

In fact, the tabernacle and all the sacrificial offerings, made by the priesthood, served to typify and prefigure Christ as our ultimate and complete sacrifice.

Isaac's carrying the wood for his own sacrifice to Mt. Moriah is a prefigure of Christ carrying the cross to Mt. Calvary.

Joseph being sold into slavery for silver is a prefigure of Christ being betrayed for the price of a slave in silver, and so forth. The rock from which Israel drank in the wilderness prefigures Christ, the rock of our salvation. (1 Cor. 10:3-4)

---

[4] @book Woo-3467, author = Wood, D. R. W.; Marshall, I. Howard, title = New Bible Dictionary, publisher = InterVarsity Press, address = Downers Grove, year = 1996, c1982, c1962, pages = 1214, keywords = Bible, edition = electronic ed. of 3rd ed., descriptor = Includes index.

The whole Old Testament is in this way telling the Christian story in advance.

A "type" is an Old Testament picture of a New Testament truth.

II. Understanding the Essential Characteristics of a Type.

"The four essential characteristics of a type are: (1) the type and the antitype must be historical persons, events, or institutions; (2) there must be some notable points of correspondence between the type and the antitype; (3) there must be an intensification of the antitype from the type; and, (4) some evidence that the type is ordained by God to foreshadow the antitype must be present. These are unchanging distinctives, which provide proper exegetical boundaries in typological interpretation. Without these four features in a passage, the pastor must be aware that typology is not likely present." [5]

It is important to understand that types do not stand-alone. Types serve to speak of the reality to come and are correctly understood in the light of their prophetic fulfillment and the clear teaching by the Apostles in the New Testament.

What God has hidden in the Scriptures through types, serves believers today, not to establish doctrine, but rather to confirm the truths taught in the New Testament to us, reassuring our hearts of God's great love and glorious purpose in Christ.

---

[5]   @book W-41, author = World Evangelical Fellowship. Theological Commission, title = Evangelical review of theology: Volume 21, publisher = Paternoster Periodicals, address = Carlisle, Cumbria, UK, year = 2000, 1997, pages = 236, volume = 21, keywords = Theology, edition = electronic ed., series-title = Logos Library System; Evangelical Review of Theology, descriptor = "A digest of articles and book reviews selected from publications worldwide for an international readership, interpreting the Christian faith for contemporary living."

III. Understanding the Importance of Typology in Preaching.

So, why is preaching typology important? As preachers, why do we bother identifying the connections between the Old and New Testaments and declaring them to the modern church audience?

"First of all, and most importantly, typology underscores the doctrine of the sovereignty of God. It teaches that the Lord has sovereignly planned history with a unified purpose so that what God has done in the past becomes the measure of the future... In other words, God has directed history so that foreshadowings occur...

Secondly, recognition of typology affirms the doctrine of the immutability of God. Typology demonstrates that God is unchanging... The typological patterns show that the way God dealt with people in the past is the way he will deal with them now and in the future. The Christian congregation can take great solace in those patterns because God will treat his people today in a similar fashion. It is incumbent upon the pastor to point out these eternal truths to his flock.

Thirdly, the principles of typology reflect the unity of Scripture. Many congregations view the Scriptures as fragmented because they have difficulty seeing how one section of the Bible relates to another. How do the poetic books relate to the gospels? Is there any association between the apocalyptic vision of John's Revelation and the Pentateuch of Moses? Such questions can be answered in the affirmative because the biblical system of typology provides homogeneity between the testaments. From every section of the Old Testament patterns are set which are later repeated and fulfilled in the New Testament.

Finally, typology adds depth and richness to the preaching message. It reveals material rarely studied or seen before, and it helps to make the Scriptures come to life. [6]

---

[6] @book W-1500, author = World Evangelical Fellowship. Theological Commission, title = Evangelical review of theology: Volume 21, publisher = Paternoster Periodicals, address = Carlisle, Cumbria, UK, year = 2000, 1997, pages = 247, volume = 21, keywords = Theology, edition = electronic ed., series-title = Logos Library System; Evangelical Review of Theology, descriptor = "A

The temptations and subsequent failures that the nation of Israel experienced in their wilderness wanderings is a clear foreshadowing of the New Testament wilderness temptation Jesus experienced and overcame.

When Israel was tested regarding **the lust of the flesh** they murmured and complained against God and Moses until God supplied an abundance of meat upon which they gorged themselves.

After Jesus completed forty days of fasting, he began to physically starve to death and at that point of desperation he was tested in the realm of his fleshly desires; however, unlike Israel, he refused to complain or endeavor to prove his Sonship. He simply reiterated the OT Scripture from <u>Deut. 8:3</u>, which says, *"…man does not live on bread alone but on every word that comes from the mouth of the Lord."*

The lust of the eyes is equated to achieving the desires, dreams, and visions of our heart.

So, when pressed from thirst, the children of Israel failed to trust God and began to murmur and complain. They questioned the reality of God's abiding presence and His willingness to bring about His stated purposes of bringing them into the land of Canaan.

When Satan took Jesus to the pinnacle of the Temple encouraging him to jump and make a spectacular entrance declaring His messiahship, it was done in order to test Jesus' faith in God's abiding presence and willingness to fulfill His promises.

Jesus responded by quoting <u>Deut. 6:16</u> – *"You shall not put the Lord your God to the test."*

The third temptation related to the issue of **supremacy**, the issue of who sits on the throne of the heart, or **the pride of life**. Israel was given the charge to not forget the Lord, but to obey His commandments, rules, and statutes. Failing to make the Lord supreme and worship Him only, they became an example for us today.

---

digest of articles and book reviews selected from publications worldwide for an international readership, interpreting the Christian faith for contemporary living."

When Jesus was tested in this area of his life with everything Satan could offer, he simply quoted Scripture from <u>Deut. 6:13</u> – *"You shall worship the Lord your God and him only shall you serve."*

The primary teaching from this type is the contrast of Jesus' obedient fulfillment of what Israel failed to obey. Israel rebelled during their wilderness testings by failing to trust in Yahweh, but Jesus was faithful to God during his wilderness testings.

The use of typology is an essential element in biblical preaching. If we shun its use in the pulpit, we risk failing to declare the great bounty and fertility of God's holy and inspired word to our congregations. Rather, we should be like Paul when he said that he *'did not shrink from proclaiming the whole counsel of God'* (<u>Acts 20:27</u>).

The types and anti-types found in Scripture were put there by God to aid our understanding of Him and His purposes, and to tie together and illuminate the two main parts of His revelation, given as it was over a period of fifteen hundred years.

In the next chapter, we begin to address the types found in 1 Samuel chapters 1-7. As we study these chapters, we will begin to gain fresh insight into the mystery of God's ways as He chooses to set us free from the influence and dominance of our sin nature.

Chapter Four

New Birth in Christ

Before reading the entire fourth chapter, acquaint yourself with Samuel's family by reading the Scriptural passage in 1 Samuel chapter one.

<u>1 Samuel 1:1-28</u> – "¹ Now there was a certain man of Ramathaim Zophim, of the mountains of Ephraim, and his name *was* Elkanah the son of Jeroham, the son of Elihu, the son of Tohu, the son of Zuph, an Ephraimite. ² And he had two wives: the name of one *was* Hannah, and the name of the other Peninnah. Peninnah had children, but Hannah had no children.

³ This man went up from his city yearly to worship and sacrifice to the Lord of hosts in Shiloh. Also the two sons of Eli, Hophni and Phinehas, the priests of the Lord, *were* there. ⁴ And whenever the time came for Elkanah to make an offering, he would give portions to Peninnah his wife and to all her sons and daughters. ⁵ But to Hannah he would give a double portion, for he loved Hannah, although the Lord had closed her womb. ⁶ And her rival also provoked her severely, to make her miserable, because the Lord had closed her womb. ⁷ So it was, year by year, when she went up to the house of the Lord, that she provoked her; therefore she wept and did not eat. ⁸ Then Elkanah her husband said to her, 'Hannah, why do you weep? Why do you not eat? And why is your heart grieved? *Am* I not better to you than ten sons?'

⁹ So Hannah arose after they had finished eating and drinking in Shiloh. Now Eli the priest was sitting on the seat by the doorpost of the tabernacle of the Lord. ¹⁰ And she *was* in bitterness of soul, and prayed to the Lord and wept in anguish. ¹¹ Then she made a vow and said, 'O Lord of hosts, if You will indeed look on the affliction of Your maidservant and remember

me, and not forget Your maidservant, but will give Your maidservant a male child, then I will give him to the Lord all the days of his life, and no razor shall come upon his head.'

[12] And it happened, as she continued praying before the Lord, that Eli watched her mouth.

[13] Now Hannah spoke in her heart; only her lips moved, but her voice was not heard. Therefore Eli thought she was drunk. [14] So Eli said to her, 'How long will you be drunk? Put your wine away from you!'

[15] And Hannah answered and said, 'No, my lord, I *am* a woman of sorrowful spirit. I have drunk neither wine nor intoxicating drink, but have poured out my soul before the Lord. [16] Do not consider your maidservant a wicked woman, for out of the abundance of my complaint and grief I have spoken until now.'

[17] Then Eli answered and said, 'Go in peace, and the God of Israel grant your petition which you have asked of Him.'

[18] And she said, 'Let your maidservant find favor in your sight.' So the woman went her way and ate, and her face was no longer *sad*.

[19] Then they rose early in the morning and worshiped before the Lord, and returned and came to their house at Ramah. And Elkanah knew Hannah his wife, and the Lord remembered her. [20] So it came to pass in the process of time that Hannah conceived and bore a son, and called his name Samuel, *saying*, 'Because I have asked for him from the Lord.'

[21] Now the man Elkanah and all his house went up to offer to the Lord the yearly sacrifice and his vow. [22] But Hannah did not go up, for she said to her husband, '*Not* until the child is weaned; then I will take him, that he may appear before the Lord and remain there forever.'

[23] And Elkanah her husband said to her, 'Do what seems best to you; wait until you have weaned him. Only let the Lord establish His word.' So the woman stayed and nursed her son until she had weaned him.

[24] Now when she had weaned him, she took him up with her, with three bulls, one ephah of flour, and a skin of wine, and brought him to the

house of the Lord in Shiloh. And the child *was* young. ²⁵ Then they slaughtered a bull, and brought the child to Eli. ²⁶ And she said, 'O my lord! As your soul lives, my lord, I *am* the woman who stood by you here, praying to the Lord. ²⁷ For this child I prayed, and the Lord has granted me my petition which I asked of Him. ²⁸ Therefore I also have lent him to the Lord; as long as he lives he shall be lent to the Lord.' So they worshiped the Lord there." (NKJV)

I. Understanding the Various Types in 1 Samuel Chapters 1-7

Understanding the typology God uses in 1 Samuel chapters 1-7 helps us understand God's ways in delivering us from the influence and domination of our sin nature. Note:

1. **Israel** is a type of **the New Testament Believer.**
2. **Samuel** is a type of **Christ.**
3. **Philistines** are a type of **the external enemy** (Satan and demonic powers).
4. **Eli** is a type of **the flesh** (the rebellious sin nature inherited from Adam).
5. **Hophni and Phinehas** (the offspring of Eli) typify the **fruits of the flesh**
   - **Hophni** (in Hebrew) = **Pugilist.** Relating to these works of the flesh (anger, envy, rage, murder, hatred, bitterness, strife, division, unforgiveness, etc.).
   - **Phinehas** (in Hebrew) = **Serpent's mouth.** Relating to these works of the flesh (lying, immorality, backbiting, gossip, slander, jealousy, filthy language, unwholesome talk, etc.)

God's Word gives us a clear picture of what our sin nature looks like so we can easily identify it as it expresses itself in our behavior. God also admonishes us in Scripture to cease identifying with our old nature and start identifying with the new nature Christ has given us.

Our behavior is to become an expression of the Holy Spirit's activity in our lives.

Gal. 5:19-21 – *"The acts of the sinful nature are obvious: sexual immorality, impurity and debauchery; idolatry and witchcraft; hatred, discord, jealousy, fits of rage, selfish ambition, dissensions, factions and envy; drunkenness, orgies, and the like. I warn you, as I did before, that those who live like this will not inherit the kingdom of God."* (NIV)

Eph. 4:22, 25, 28-31 – *"You were taught, with regard to your former way of life, to put off your old self, which is being corrupted by its deceitful desires; to be made new in the attitude of your minds. Therefore each of you must put off falsehood and speak truthfully to his neighbor, for we are all members of one body. He who has been stealing must steal no longer, but must work. Do not let any unwholesome talk come out of your mouths, but only what is helpful for building others up according to their needs, that it may benefit those who listen. Do not grieve the Holy Spirit of God, with whom you were sealed for the day of redemption. Get rid of all bitterness, rage and anger, brawling and slander, along with every form of malice."* (NIV)

Col. 3:5-9 – *"Put to death, therefore, whatever belongs to your earthly nature; sexual immorality, impurity, lust, evil desires and greed, which is idolatry. Because of these, the wrath of God is coming. You used to walk in these ways, in the life you once lived. But now you must rid yourselves of all such things as these: anger, rage, malice, slander, and filthy language from your lips. Do not lie to each other, since you have taken off your old self with its practices and have put on the new self, which is being renewed in knowledge in the image of its Creator."* (NIV)

The message of Scripture is quite clear – Get rid of your former way of life and put off your old self, which has been corrupted by its deceitful desires. Behavior that gives expression to your fallen Adamic nature is not acceptable to your heavenly Father.

So, God is expecting each new believer to draw upon the new life of Christ within his spirit and obey the Word of God in the Bible, on which every believer is to be consistently feeding. Only in this way will he receive the mind of Christ and be able to express the very life of Christ.

The apostle Paul tells us that *"At one time you were separated from God. You were his enemies in your minds, and the evil things you did were against God."* **Col. 1:21** (NCV)

Prior to new birth in Jesus Christ, we were all enemies of God because of our thought life and sinful behavior. Following the experience of personal regeneration in our spirit, the apostle Paul exhorts us to become progressively changed or "transformed" in the way we think by having our minds renewed by the word of God.

This book focuses on understanding the divine process of spiritual transformation – the "saving of the soul." It unveils the process God uses in the lives of New Testament believers: first, to uncover and expose our sinful behavior so that the enemy's strongholds in our lives will be revealed; and second, to deliver us from those fleshly strongholds.

It is through an uncontrolled outburst of anger that we are able to recognize that the enemy has established a stronghold of anger in our lives. It is only as we die to trying to live victoriously in our own strength and cry out for deliverance that the revelation of Jesus Christ, imparted to us by the Holy Spirit, actually allows us to live in victory over our flesh and the enemy's attacks. I will share more on this in later chapters.

II. Israel's Spiritual Condition prior to the Birth of Samuel

Prior to Samuel's entrance on the scene in Israel's history, God had periodically raised up Judges to administrate the Law-word of God and govern Israel; however, by the time Samuel was born, the nation had degenerated both morally and politically.

Gal. 3:24 – *"Wherefore the law was our schoolmaster to bring us unto Christ, that we might be justified by faith."* (KJV)

The New Testament gives us insight regarding the purpose of the Law. One function of the Law was to harness the people and keep them from wandering away from God and help prepare them for the coming of Messiah; however, it was inadequate in producing God's righteousness in the hearts of the people.

Due to the lack of God's Word being effectively proclaimed and upheld by the priesthood, the Tabernacle for God's presence at Shiloh had been desecrated and the priesthood had fallen into corruption and immorality.

As New Testament believers, the apostle Paul helps us understand that an additional purpose of the Law of God is to reveal the fallen condition of our hearts. Even though we may try to obey God's Word, endeavoring to be as good as possible, we still commit sinful acts in attitude, speech, and deeds. Thus, God's perfect Law helps us recognize that something is wrong with our heart.

Rom. 3:20, 23 – *"For no one can ever be made right with God by doing what the law commands. The law simply shows us how sinful we are. For everyone has sinned; we all fall short of God's glorious standard."* (NLT)

Jer. 17:9-10 – *"The human heart is the most deceitful of all things, and desperately wicked. Who really knows how bad it is? But I, the Lord, search all hearts and examine secret motives. I give all people their due rewards, according to what their actions deserve."* (NLT)

In this portion of Scripture in first Samuel, the nation of Israel is a type of the New Testament believer and represents the spiritual condition that we all face prior to being born again by the Spirit of the Living God. No one comes to Jesus to be saved without first realizing that they are a sinner and need to be saved. It is upon realizing the corrupt and vile condition of our own hearts that we become willing to surrender to Christ asking for His forgiveness and cleansing.

Many modern day Christians grew up within a religious environment, which tends to make them think that because they are 'good' moral people they don't need to be saved; however, God's goal for mankind exceeds our being 'good' in our own eyes. We have all partaken of the tree of the knowledge of good and evil and thus, all capable of good and evil. But our goodness is as filthy rags in God's holy sight.

God's purpose is nothing less than every redeemed person being truly conformed to the image of Christ, which is only possible as we share His holy nature.

III. Understanding Elkanah's Religious Heritage and Family Situation

Like Elkanah, many Christians are born into a family with an extensive religious heritage. Let's look at Elkanah's religious heritage.

Throughout the Bible we find that God places special emphasis on the names of people and places. After his character-changing encounter with God, **Jacob** (meaning "supplanter") received a name change to **Israel** (meaning "prince with God"). In the same way, Saul of Tarsus was renamed Paul after his divine encounter and resultant salvation (<u>Acts 9:1-19</u>).

It is important to note that the name a person receives at birth does not always express the reality of what they are at birth, or more significantly, what kind of a person they can become as they encounter God's holy presence and seek to fulfill God's purpose in their lives.

Verse 1 – *"Now there was a certain man of Ramathaim Zophim, of the mountains of Ephraim, and his name was Elkanah the son of Jeroham, the son of Elihu, the son of Tohu, the son of Zuph, an Ephraimite."* (NKJV)

Person
Tohu = "Lowly" (Great-great grandfather)
Elihu = "He is my God" (Great grandfather)
Jeroham = "One who is loved" (Grandfather)
Elkanah = "Possessed by God" (Father of Samuel)

Place
Ramathaim = "Heavenlies"
Zophim = "Watchers"
Ephraim = "Fruitful Place"

Everything recorded in the word of God has purpose. Everything God does is with purpose. This list of names is not given to us by God simply to establish a historical setting, although they provide that service. Instead, these names are given to provide us with spiritual insight.

What a tremendous heritage for Samuel. A great-great grandfather who, if he fulfilled the prophetic significance of his name, walked in humility before the Lord, a great grandfather who honored God by bearing witness through his allegiance to God, a grandfather who expressed God's love and was loved by others, and a father who belonged to and worshiped the living God. They lived in a mountainous region that was known as a spiritually fruitful place because the people had a heavenly perspective watching for God's activity in the earth.

What this passage teaches us is that we can be raised in seemingly the best possible environment and still fail to walk perfectly before the Lord. Here we see Elkanah copying Abraham's mistake in his desire to have children. Apparently not able to have children with Hannah, Elkanah was unable to wait for God's timing and so, married a second wife named Peninnah.

The spiritual heritage of Elkanah's family was insufficient to meet the moral need represented in the nation of Israel, and the spiritual heritage we may receive from our family will not be sufficient to save us.

On the national level, Israel needed nothing less than a godly prophet to bring God's Word to the people, and on a personal level, we need nothing less than to be 'born again,' to have the life of Christ personally birthed within us so that we may come to know the word of God on a personal level.

The family situation:

Verse 2 – *"Elkanah had two wives named Hannah and Peninnah. Peninnah had children, but Hannah had none."* (NCV)

Elkanah had two wives. One of the family traditions in that day, due to the strong emphasis on having children, was to marry a second wife if the first wife, for whatever reason, couldn't bear children.

The important thing to see here is that God takes the inequities, limitations, and difficulties of life and makes them work for our good and His divine purposes.

> Even if we grow up in a religious family, worshiping God on a regular basis, and are shown love in a variety of ways, we still need life from God in order to fill up the spiritual emptiness deep within.

Through Hannah, we see the plight of every person prior to receiving redemption and new life in Christ. Our spiritual condition is one of barrenness and others who are bearing fruit and successful in life, serve to provoke us to jealousy and encourage us to press into God for spiritual fruitfulness in our own lives.

Verses 3-5 – *"This man went up from his city yearly to worship and sacrifice to the LORD of hosts in Shiloh. Also the two sons of Eli, Hophni and Phinehas, the priests of the LORD, were there. And whenever the time came for Elkanah to make an offering, he would give portions to Peninnah his wife and to all her sons and daughters. But to Hannah he would give a double portion, for he loved Hannah, although the LORD had closed her womb."*

Being loved and cared for in the natural is definitely a comfort, but it does not make you satisfied in your inner man. Physical satisfaction or emotional comfort does not equate to spiritual fulfillment. Elkanah loved Hannah, but that never appeased or freed her from her God-given desire to have children. Like Hannah, each one of us needs a personal encounter with God so we can receive life from above.

IV. Comprehending the Need For Delay to Produce Brokenness:

James 4:2 – *"The reason you don't have what you want is that you don't ask God for it."* (NLT)

Hannah didn't have that problem; in fact, year after year she approached the Lord in prayer asking God to give her a child. But her prayers went unanswered.

Often delay is a means that God uses to work in our heart and lead us into brokenness, as well as to work out perfect timing in the circumstances around us. Sometimes the delay is present because we are asking with the wrong motives.

James 4:3 – *"And even when you do ask, you don't get it because your whole motive is wrong—you want only what will give you pleasure."*

So, just asking God for what you want doesn't always get you what you want.

Isa. 57:15 – *"For this is what the high and lofty One says— he who lives forever, whose name is holy: 'I live in a high and holy place, but also with him who is contrite and lowly in spirit, to revive the spirit of the lowly and to revive the heart of the contrite.'"* (NIV)

What we find is that it wasn't until Hannah became utterly broken and contrite in her spirit and then fasted and prayed in deep desperation that she caught a vision beyond her own personal desire for a child. She touched the heart of God and saw God's need for a prophet in the land and then she began to pray for a son, which included the promise to give him back to the Lord.

Brokenness and desperation were the blessings of God's grace, which enabled Hannah to become willing to make the sacrifice of giving Samuel back to God.

God's need was for a prophet in the land. So, until Hannah prayed according to the will of God, her prayer went unanswered. But once Hannah prayed, **according to the will of God**, asking for God's need to be met, then God answered her prayer, opening her womb and giving her the desire of her heart.

1 John 5:14-15 – *"This is the confidence we have in approaching God: that if we ask anything **according to his will**, he hears us. And if we know that he hears us – whatever we ask – we know that we have what we asked of him."* (NIV)

Our ability to cease praying for selfish reasons only comes when we have become broken and contrite before God. Brokenness is a state of absolute surrender to God's will, which enables us to die to our own will and obey the Holy Spirit's direction.

V. New Birth in Christ – The Answer to
Desperate Prayer

Verses 17-28 – Although Eli was carnal and fleshly as a priest; he carried the responsibility of being God's representative and spoke on behalf of the Lord. So, when he told Hannah to "Go in peace, and may the Lord grant your petition," he was confirming God's provision for Hannah.

She received that word of confirmation and responded with a request for God's unmerited favor (grace).

Eph. 2:8-9 – *"For it is by grace you have been saved, through faith   and this not from yourselves, it is the gift of God – not by works, so that no one can boast."* (NIV)

And at that point, her face was no longer sad. Faith had entered her heart and she returned home with a whole new confidence, determined to believe God for a miracle. Being physically intimate with her husband is something Hannah had experienced on numerous occasions, but this time God was involved and His involvement makes all the difference.

Verse 19 – *"Early the next morning they arose and worshiped before the Lord and then went back to their home at Ramah. Elkanah lay with Hannah his wife, and the Lord remembered her."* (NIV)

Without God's activity in our lives we will never become pregnant with new life, no matter how many religious activities we perform.

John 1:12-13 – *"But to all who believed him and accepted him, he gave the right to become children of God. They are reborn—not with a physical birth resulting from human passion or plan, but a birth that comes from God."* (NLT)

Samuel was the evidence of new life from above. As Samuel was birthed into Israel through God's divine activity, so we are born into the kingdom of God through His divine activity.

And once we are born-again into God's kingdom, we must be nurtured for a time until we are weaned from the milk of God's Word and able to eat and digest God's Word on our own.

In addressing the believers at Corinth, the Apostle Paul explained to them that he couldn't feed them the meat of the Word because they were still babes.

1 Cor. 3:2-3a – *"I had to feed you with milk and not with solid food, because you couldn't handle anything stronger. And you still aren't ready, for you are still controlled by your own sinful desires."* (NLT)

1 Peter 2:2 – *"Desire God's pure word as newborn babies desire milk. Then you will grow in your salvation."* (GW)

VI. The Weaning of Samuel

1 Samuel 1:21-22 – *"The next year Elkanah and his family went on their annual trip to offer a sacrifice to the Lord. But Hannah did not go. She told her husband, 'Wait until the boy is weaned. Then I will take him to the Tabernacle and leave him there with the Lord permanently.'"* (NLT)

Every new believer is in reality a babe in Christ, carnal and fleshly, whether they want that to be the case or not. We all need nurturing from mature believers and to be taught by the Holy Spirit, before we can adequately function in ministry. So, don't seek to avoid that process. Be willing to be discipled or mentored by other mature believers who love Christ and are following Him closely.

Becoming a committed member in a local Bible-believing church is essential for spiritual growth.

1 Cor. 3:1-3 – *"Brothers, I could not address you as spiritual but as worldly—mere infants in Christ. I gave you milk, not solid food, for you were not yet ready for it. Indeed, you are still not ready. You are still worldly. For since there is jealousy and quarreling among you, are you not worldly? Are you not acting like mere men?"* (NIV)

Gal. 4:1-2 – *"Now I say that the heir, as long as he is a child, does not differ at all from a slave, though he is master of all, but is under guardians and stewards until the time appointed by the father."* (NKJV)

The implications of being a babe in Christ and spiritually immature means that even though we are children of the Most High God and heirs of all things in Christ, we live as though we were slaves because of the limited revelation of Christ, as our very life. So, until we receive sufficient revelation from God, we are lovingly put under the care and tutelage of pastors and other mature believers until the time appointed by the Father.

Every one of us face desperate times and negative circumstances in which we need God's divine intervention. Trying to handle these uncontrollable situations on our own can simply lead to spiritual failure and the manifestation of our carnal nature. When we turn to God and allow Him to reveal the heart of Christ to us, we can then begin to pray according to God's will and not simply pray for our own pleasure or aggrandizement.

Regardless of our family upbringing, we all need a personal encounter with God in order to experience the miracle of new life. If you are walking in your own ways, know that spiritual barrenness will be one of the consequences you will experience.

God wants to teach you **His** ways, which supersede our ways. Just think – His ways are perfect! (Psa. 18:30)

Turn your life over to Him and pray for grace to walk in **His** ways. It all begins with Jesus – He is the Way, the Truth and the Life, no one comes to the Father except through him.

Type:
1 Sam. 2:26 – *"And the boy Samuel continued to grow in stature and in favor with the Lord and with men."* (NIV)

Antitype:
Luke 2:40, 52 – *"And the child grew and became strong; he was filled with wisdom, and the grace of God was upon him. And Jesus grew in wisdom and stature, and in favor with God and men."* (NIV)

By comparing these two Scriptures, it is easy to see how Samuel is a type of Christ.

Growing in Christ or maturing as a believer – how does that happen? In the next chapter we begin to answer that question as God's Word gives us insight and understanding.

CHAPTER FIVE

Learning God's Ways as a New Believer

1 Samuel 2:1-11 – *"Hannah prayed: 'The Lord has filled my heart with joy; I feel very strong in the Lord. I can laugh at my enemies; I am glad because you have helped me! 'There is no one holy like the Lord. There is no God but you; there is no Rock like our God. 'Don't continue bragging, don't speak proud words. The Lord is a God who knows everything, and he judges what people do. 'The bows of warriors break, but weak people become strong. Those who once had plenty of food now must work for food, but people who were hungry are hungry no more. The woman who could not have children now has seven, but the woman who had many children now is sad. 'The Lord sends death, and he brings to life. He sends people to the grave, and he raises them to life again. The Lord raises the poor up from the dust, and he lifts the needy from the ashes. He lets the poor sit with princes and receive a throne of honor. 'The foundations of the earth belong to the Lord, and the Lord set the world upon them. He protects those who are loyal to him, but evil people will be silenced in darkness. Power is not the key to success. The Lord destroys his enemies; he will thunder in heaven against them. The Lord will judge all the earth. He will give power to his king and make his appointed king strong.'*

Then Elkanah went home to Ramah, but the boy continued to serve the Lord under Eli the priest." (NCV)

Every new believer in Christ experiences the amazing joy that comes as we begin to comprehend the wonder of our salvation in Christ and start to receive a revelation of the character of our heavenly Father. Hannah begins this second chapter by expressing her overflowing joy at God's divine intervention into her life and the miraculous transformation she has experienced in answer to her desperate cry.

It is important that we grasp the concept of **God's ways** versus **our ways**. How can we please God with the way we live unless we are hearing His voice and receiving His Word brought to our hearts by the Holy Spirit? For without faith, it is impossible to please God. And we know that faith only comes if we have hearing ears and are hearing the Word of God. (Heb. 11:6) (Rom. 10:17)

Deut. 10:12 – *"And now, Israel, what does the Lord your God require from you, but to fear the Lord your God, to **walk in all His ways** and love Him, and to serve the Lord your God with all your heart and with all your soul."* (NASB)

Now, we may think, "That ought to be easy enough." But there is one slight problem. God says:

Isa. 55:8-9 – *" 'My thoughts are completely different from yours,' says the Lord. 'And my ways are far beyond anything you could imagine. For just as the heavens are higher than the earth, **so are my ways higher than your ways** and my thoughts higher than your thoughts.' "* (NLT)

Understanding the majesty of God's ways is not some easy task we can perform on our own. We must depend on the Holy Spirit to teach us His ways. Failing to depend on the Holy Spirit forces us to ask the question: What happens when we walk in **our** ways, instead of walking in **God's** ways?

Deut. 28:28-29 – *"The Lord will strike you with madness and blindness and confusion of heart. And you shall grope at noonday, as a blind man gropes in darkness; you shall **not** prosper in **your** ways; you shall be only oppressed and plundered continually, and no one shall save you."* (NKJV)

Every step that America takes, moving away from God and submission to His holy Word, only brings the fulfillment of this Scripture closer. We only have to look at the consequences that have begun to plague this country, since prayer was removed from the public state-run schools in 1963, to envision the destructive end of this path.

When you look at the alternative, you can understand why the Psalmist prayed:

Psalm 25:4 – *"Show me **your** ways, O Lord, teach me **your** paths."* (NIV)

It's as we come before His presence and seek to be taught of the Lord, learning His ways, that we receive the grace to obey Him.

Isaiah 2:3 – *"Many nations will come and say, 'Come, let us go up to the mountain of the Lord, to the Temple of the God of Israel. There **he will teach us his ways, so that we may obey him.**'"* (NLT)

I. The Joy of Growing Up in Christ as a New Believer

2 Peter 1:2-4 – *"May God bless you with his special favor and wonderful peace as you **come to know Jesus**, our God and Lord, **better and better**. As we know Jesus better, his divine power gives us everything we need for living a godly life. He has called us to receive his own glory and goodness! And by that same mighty power, he has given us all of his rich and wonderful promises. He has promised that you will escape the decadence all around you caused by evil desires and that you will share in his divine nature."* (NLT)

Peter says we receive everything we need for living a godly life as we come to know Jesus better and better, partaking of His nature. That knowledge comes progressively to us as the Holy Spirit takes the things of Christ and reveals them to us.

Jesus said, *"There is so much more I want to tell you, but you can't bear it now. When the Spirit of truth comes, He will guide you into all truth. He will not speak on His own but will tell you what He has heard. He will tell you about the future. He will bring me glory by telling you whatever he receives from me."* **John 16:12-14**

2 Cor. 3:18 – *"And we all, with unveiled face, beholding the glory (the manifest character and very nature) of the Lord, are being transformed into the same image from one degree of glory to another. For this comes from the Lord who is the Spirit."* (ESV)

Eph. 4:11-16 – *"He (Jesus) is the one who gave these gifts to the church: the apostles, the prophets, the evangelists, and the pastors and teachers. Their responsibility is to equip God's people to do his work and build up the church,* *the body of Christ, until we come to such unity in our faith and knowledge of God's Son that we will **be mature and full grown in the Lord**, measuring up to the full stature of Christ.*

*Then we will **no longer** be **like children**, forever changing our minds about what we believe because someone has told us something different or because someone has cleverly lied to us and made the lie sound like the truth. Instead, we will hold to the truth in love, **becoming more and more in every way like Christ**, who is the head of his body, the church. Under his direction, the whole body is fitted together perfectly. As each part does its own special work, it helps the other parts grow, so that the whole body is healthy and growing and full of love."* (NLT)

Christ has given the 5-fold ministry gifts to the church to equip the saints to do God's work in the earth, and in addition, He has given these ministry gifts so that together we may grow up to know Christ in fullness.

So, how does this happen in the practical everyday experience of our lives? Paul teaches us:

Eph. 4:17-24 – *"So I tell you this, and insist on it in the Lord, that you must no longer live as the Gentiles do, in the futility of their thinking. They are darkened in their understanding and separated from the life of God because of the ignorance that is in them due to the hardening of their hearts. Having lost all sensitivity, they have given themselves over to sensuality so as to indulge in every kind of impurity, with a continual lust for more.*

You, however, did not come to know Christ that way. Surely you heard of him and were taught in him in accordance with the truth that is in Jesus. You were taught, with regard to your former way of life, to put off your old self, which is being corrupted by its deceitful desires; to be made new in the attitude of your minds; and to put on the new self, created to be like God in true righteousness and holiness." (NIV)

What we need to realize is that the apostle Paul, under the anointing of the Holy Spirit is writing to the Church of Jesus Christ in Ephesus. He is writing to believers admonishing them to no longer live as the Gentiles do. In other words, believers can continue living their lives out of futile thinking instead of living according to God's thoughts. Believers can live before God with darkened understanding and actually be cut off from

God's life in Jesus because of their ignorance concerning God's ways and because of a hardened heart.

How does that condition get changed? How do we learn of Christ and appropriate His life?

Interestingly, when God works to teach us Christ, He first, exposes our carnal nature by turning up the heat allowing us to get pressured beyond our ability to control. In this way, we are no longer allowed to live in denial or remain stagnant in our spiritual growth.

We may become angry and explode in a temper tantrum, become jealous, or even be drawn into sinful behavior by the lust of our eyes or the lust of our flesh, in whatever way the exposure happens, God in love is exposing our need for experiencing the fullness of the victorious life of Christ.

In response to the exposure of sinful attitudes and behavior in our lives, we often seek to cover up, control ourselves, and stifle this sinful behavior, but we do it in the energy of the flesh, and without success. Then, realizing the limitation of our abilities, in brokenness and desperation, we cry out for God to grace us and deliver us.

God's response to our cry for help is to give us a fresh revelation of Jesus as our victory. Once we learn how to start drawing upon His life and strength, we experience victory over the previous sinful behavior and are actually able to put off the sinful attitude and behavior and put on the expression of Christ in righteousness and holiness.

Eph. 4:22 – *"Since, then, we do not have the excuse of ignorance, everything— and I do mean everything—connected with that old way of life has to go. It's rotten through and through. Get rid of it! And then take on an entirely new way of life—a God-fashioned life, a life renewed from the inside and working itself into your conduct as God accurately reproduces his character in you."* (Msg)

Galatians 6:8 – *"If you plant in (the soil of) your corrupt nature, you will harvest destruction. But if you plant in (the soil of) your spiritual nature, you will harvest everlasting life."* (GW)

When we are born of the Holy Spirit, the spirit of Christ takes up residence in our human spirit, which was dead in sins. The entrance of the Holy Spirit makes us alive unto God and we begin to learn what it means to worship God in spirit and in truth. However, in order to be acceptable in the way we worship God, we must learn **His ways**.

II. Reasons and Occasions for Rejoicing in the Lord

Throughout the New Testament we find a variety of reasons and occasions for rejoicing in the Lord: His incarnation; His power; His presence; His ultimate triumph; our names written in the Lamb's book of life; the harvest; suffering for the cause of Christ and the gospel; etc; but the greatest reason is our own personal redemption and salvation in Christ.

The birth of Samuel in Israel is a type of Christ being born in us through the regenerating work of the Holy Spirit. Once Samuel was born into Israel, Hannah rejoiced in the Lord.   In the same way, we are to rejoice in the new revelation we receive of God's grace and mercy.

1 Sam. 2:1-2 – *"And Hannah prayed and said, 'My heart exults in the Lord; my strength is exalted in the Lord. My mouth derides my enemies, because I rejoice in your salvation. 'There is none holy like the Lord; there is none besides you; there is no rock like our God.' "* (ESV)

In the same way, David rejoiced in God's saving deliverance: *"I will praise the Lord at all times. I will constantly speak his praises. I will boast only in the Lord; let all who are discouraged take heart. Come, let us tell of the Lord's greatness; let us exalt his name together. I prayed to the Lord, and he answered me, freeing me from all my fears. Those who look to him for help will be radiant with joy; no shadow of shame will darken their faces. I cried out to the Lord in my suffering, and he heard me. He set me free from all my fears. For the angel of the Lord guards all who fear him, and he rescues them. Taste and see that the Lord is good. Oh, the joys of those who trust in him! Let the Lord's people show him reverence, for those who honor him will have all they need. Even strong young lions sometimes go hungry, but those who trust in the Lord will never lack any good thing."* Psalm 34:1-10 (NLT)

The Scriptures instruct us in how we are to express our worship of the Lord and that includes expressing our joy in being saved, and doing so, with exuberance!! You simply cannot "shout with joy" in a calm or passive way.

Psalm 100:1-4 – "***Shout with joy*** *to the Lord, O earth! Worship the Lord* ***with gladness***. *Come before him,* ***singing with joy***. *Acknowledge that the Lord is God! He made us, and we are his. We are his people, the sheep of his pasture. Enter his gates with* ***thanksgiving***; *go into his courts with* ***praise***. *Give thanks to him and bless his name.*" (NLT)

Psalm 107:22 – "*Let them offer sacrifices of thanksgiving and* ***sing joyfully*** *about his glorious acts.*" (NLT)

Psalm 5:11 – "*But let all who take refuge in you* ***be glad***; *let them ever* ***sing for joy***. *Spread your protection over them, that those who love your name may* ***rejoice in you***." (NIV)

Psalm 95:1 – "*Come, let us* ***sing for joy*** *to the Lord; let us shout aloud to the Rock of our salvation.*" (NIV)

Col. 3:16 – "*Let the Word of Christ—the Message—have the run of the house. Give it plenty of room in your lives. Instruct and direct one another using good common sense. And sing,* ***sing your hearts out*** *to God!*" (Msg)

Phil. 4:4 – "***Rejoice*** *in the Lord always. I will say it again:* ***Rejoice!***" (NIV)

Luke 19:6-10 – "*Zacchaeus quickly climbed down and took Jesus to his house* ***in great excitement and joy***. *But the crowds were displeased. 'He has gone to be the guest of a notorious sinner,' they grumbled.*

Meanwhile, Zacchaeus stood there and said to the Lord, 'I will give half my wealth to the poor, Lord, and if I have overcharged people on their taxes, I will give them back four times as much!'

*Jesus responded, '****Salvation has come*** *to this home today, for this man has shown himself to be a son of Abraham. And I, the Son of Man, have come to seek and save those like him who are lost.'*"

Romans 4:7-8 – "*Oh,* ***what joy*** *for those whose disobedience is forgiven, whose sins are put out of sight.* ***Yes, what joy*** *for those whose sin is no longer counted against them by the Lord.*"

Luke 15:10 — *"There is **joy** in the presence of God's angels when even one sinner repents."*

Romans 14:17 – *"For the kingdom of God is not a matter of eating and drinking, but of righteousness, peace and **joy in the Holy Spirit**."* (NIV)

When we gather as believers, our gatherings should reflect an exuberant joy as we rejoice in what Christ has accomplished on our behalf. Our vision should be off of ourselves and lifted up beholding His glory and majesty. Our voices should be raised declaring the wonder of His marvelous grace. God loves us with an unconditional love and He is committed to completing our redemption by sharing His very life with us in and through the Lord Jesus Christ.

Neither Elizabeth nor Mary could refrain from expressing their joy at the arrival of Jesus, God's salvation.

Luke 1:43-55 – *"What an honor this is, that the mother of my Lord should visit me! When you came in and greeted me, my baby jumped for joy the instant I heard your voice! You are blessed, because you believed that the Lord would do what he said.*

*Mary responded, 'Oh, how I praise the Lord. **How I rejoice in God my Savior!** For he took notice of his lowly servant girl, and now generation after generation will call me blessed. For he, the Mighty One, is holy, and he has done great things for me. His mercy goes on from generation to generation, to all who fear him. His mighty arm does tremendous things! How he scatters the proud and haughty ones! He has taken princes from their thrones and exalted the lowly. He has satisfied the hungry with good things and sent the rich away with empty hands. And how he has helped his servant Israel! He has not forgotten his promise to be merciful. For he promised our ancestors—Abraham and his children—to be merciful to them forever.'"* (NLT)

Mary's rejoicing and verbal praise reminds us of the earlier praise in 1 Samuel 2:11.

III. Hannah's Rejoicing in the Personal Revelation of God's Character

1 Sam. 2:1-10 – *"Then Hannah prayed: 'My heart rejoices in the Lord! Oh, how the Lord has blessed me! Now I have an answer for my enemies, as I delight in your deliverance.*

[2] No one is holy like the Lord! There is no one besides you; there is no Rock like our God.

[3] "Stop acting so proud and haughty! Don't speak with such arrogance! The Lord is a God who knows your deeds; and he will judge you for what you have done.

[4] Those who were mighty are mighty no more; and those who were weak are now strong.

[5] Those who were well fed are now starving; and those who were starving are now full. The barren woman now has seven children; but the woman with many children will have no more.

[6] The Lord brings both death and life; he brings some down to the grave but raises others up.

[7] The Lord makes one poor and another rich; he brings one down and lifts another up.

[8] He lifts the poor from the dust—yes, from a pile of ashes! He treats them like princes, placing them in seats of honor. 'For all the earth is the Lord's, and he has set the world in order.

[9] He will protect his godly ones, but the wicked will perish in darkness. No one will succeed by strength alone.

[10] Those who fight against the Lord will be broken. He thunders against them from heaven; the Lord judges throughout the earth. He gives mighty strength to his king; he increases the might of his anointed one." (NLT)

With the bursting forth of new life, Hannah (who is an example of one who has received new life in Christ) is blessed with fresh insight and revelation from God. This new insight and understanding concerning God's character and God's ways is reflected in her prophetic declaration.

1. One of the first realizations we experience when receiving Christ, as Savior, is freedom from guilt and internal peace. This results in great rejoicing and exaltation in the Lord for His gracious salvation. (1 Sam.2:1)

Acts 13:39 – *"Everyone who believes in him is freed from all guilt and declared right with God – something the Jewish law could never do."*

2. We realize there is none to compare to the Lord our rock. He alone is holy. (1 Sam.2:2)

1 Cor. 10:4 – *"For they all drank from the miraculous rock that traveled with them, and that rock was Christ."*

3. We realize there is no place for pride or arrogance because God is the judge of all our words. (1 Sam.2:3)

Matt. 16:27 – *"For I, the Son of Man, will come in the glory of my Father with his angels and will judge all people according to their deeds."*

4. We realize there are real consequences for a prideful heart – the mighty are broken and stumble. The full go away hungry; however, walking in humility, the barren become fruitful. (1 Sam.2:4)

5. We recognize the Lord can bring you low or lift you up. He is the Lord! (1 Sam.2:5, 8)

Deut. 32:39 – *"Don't you understand? I am the only God; there are no others. I am the one who takes life and gives it again. I punished you with suffering. But now I will heal you, and nothing can stop me!"* (CEV)

6. He preserves His saints, but the wicked end up in darkness; for by human strength shall no man prevail. God's enemies are shattered, but He gives strength to His anointed. (1 Sam.2:9)

1 Cor. 1:26-27 – *"Remember, dear brothers and sisters, that few of you were wise in the world's eyes, or powerful, or wealthy when God called you. Instead, God deliberately chose things the world considers foolish in order to shame those who think they are wise. And he chose those who are powerless to shame those who are powerful."* (NLT)

Not only did the Lord deliver Hannah from her barrenness, but He also made her a fruitful vine by giving her three more boys and two girls. (1 Sam. 2:21)

Literally scores of Scriptures, in both the Old and New Testament, talk of the importance of rejoicing in the presence of the Lord. When presenting their offerings to the Lord at the three required Feasts, the children of Israel were **commanded** to **rejoice in the Lord**.

Deut. 16:1-2, 8-17 – *"In honor of the Lord your God, always **celebrate** the Passover at the proper time in early spring… For the next six days you may not eat bread made with yeast. On the seventh day the people must assemble before the Lord your God, and no work may be done on that day.*

*Count off seven weeks from the beginning of your grain harvest. Then you must **celebrate** the Festival of Harvest (Pentecost) to honor the Lord your God. Bring him a freewill offering in proportion to the blessings you have received from him… **Celebrate** with your whole family… Another celebration, the Festival of Shelters, must be observed for seven days at the end of the harvest season, after the grain has been threshed and the grapes have been pressed. This festival will be **a happy time of rejoicing**… For seven days **celebrate** this festival to honor the Lord your God at the place he chooses, for it is the Lord your God who gives you bountiful harvests and blesses all your work. This festival will be **a time of great joy for all**.*

*Each year every man in Israel **must celebrate** these three festivals: the Festival of Unleavened Bread (Passover), the Festival of Harvest (Pentecost), and the Festival of Shelters (Tabernacles). They must appear before the Lord your God at the place he chooses on each of these occasions, and they must bring a gift to the Lord. All must give as they are able, according to the blessings given to them by the Lord your God."* (NLT)

If you have lost your joy, it is time to repent and pray for the restoration of your joy, so that you may worship in spirit and in truth.

Psalm 51:8, 12 – *"Oh, give me back my **joy** again; you have broken me—now let me rejoice… Restore to me again the **joy** of your salvation, and make me willing to obey you."* (NLT)

Having observed the glorious response of worship by Hannah in which she glorified the Lord, rejoicing in her salvation, we realize the kind of response we should experience as we grow in the realization of our own glorious redemption.

1 Samuel 2:11 – *"... The boy Samuel stayed in Shiloh and served the Lord **under** the priest Eli."* (TEV)

As a born-again believer, two natures reside within us: the one we received from Adam and the new nature we have received from Christ, the federal head of the New Creation.

From this verse, as well as from New Testament passages, we see that although we are born again and have a new nature from Christ living in us, we may still be serving our flesh nature (Eli) in the way we worship and serve God. (Rom. 7:17; Gal. 5:17)

If that is the case, we will find ourselves offering soulish and even hypocritical worship to God.

2 Tim. 3:1-5 – *"You should also know this, Timothy, that in the last days there will be very difficult times. For people will love only themselves and their money. They will be boastful and proud, scoffing at God, disobedient to their parents, and ungrateful. They will consider nothing sacred. They will be unloving and unforgiving; they will slander others and have no self-control; they will be cruel and have no interest in what is good. They will betray their friends, be reckless, be puffed up with pride, and **love pleasure rather than God**. They will act as if they are religious, but **they will reject the power** that could make them godly. You must stay away from people like that."*

What we may not fully realize, at this point in our growth in Christ, is that in many ways our soul (mind, will, and emotions) is already conformed to the ideologies and philosophies promoted by the world-system. Our need, as the apostle Paul points out in Romans 12:1-2 is to be transformed by the renewing of our mind; and yet, if we are ignorant of God's will and God's ways and still conformed to the world-system, our flesh will seek to negatively influence our ability to offer pure worship to God.

Without a renewed mind, we will end up loving pleasure rather than God and rejecting the power of the gospel to truly make people godly. Know that religious activity will never please God, only worship that is initiated by the Holy Spirit, rising out of our human spirit, and in Truth (agreement with the revelation of God's Word) will be pleasing in His sight.

We now turn to see what happens when the fruits of the flesh (Hophni and Phinehas) influence our desire to offer pure worship to God.

CHAPTER SIX

Self-centered Worship is Unacceptable

1 Samuel 2:11 – *"... The boy Samuel stayed in Shiloh and served the Lord **under** the priest Eli."* (TEV)

I. God's Way is to Consume the Fat – Therefore, Self-centered Worship is Unacceptable to God

1 Sam. 1:12-25 – *"Now the sons of Eli were scoundrels who had no respect for the Lord or for their duties as priests. Whenever anyone offered a sacrifice, Eli's sons would send over a servant with a three-pronged fork. While the meat of the sacrificed animal was still boiling, the servant would stick the fork into the pot and demand that whatever it brought up be given to Eli's sons. All the Israelites who came to worship at Shiloh were treated this way. Sometimes the servant would come even **before the animal's fat had been burned** on the altar. He would demand raw meat before it had been boiled so that it could be used for roasting.*

*The man offering the sacrifice might reply, 'Take as much as you want, but **the fat must first be burned**.' Then the servant would demand, 'No, give it to me now, or I'll take it by force.' So the sin of these young men was very serious in the Lord's sight, for **they treated the Lord's offerings with contempt**.*

Now Samuel, though only a boy, was the Lord's helper. He wore a linen tunic just like that of a priest. Each year his mother made a small coat for him and brought it to him when she came with her husband for the sacrifice. Before they returned home, Eli would bless Elkanah and his wife and say, 'May the

*Lord give you other children to take the place of this one she gave to the Lord.'
And the Lord gave Hannah three sons and two daughters. Meanwhile, Samuel
grew up in the presence of the Lord.*

*Now Eli was very old, but he was aware of what his sons were doing to the
people of Israel. He knew, for instance, that his sons were seducing the young
women who assisted at the entrance of the Tabernacle. Eli said to them, 'I have
been hearing reports from the people about the wicked things you are doing.
Why do you keep sinning? You must stop, my sons! The reports I hear among
the Lord's people are not good. If someone sins against another person, God
can mediate for the guilty party. But if someone sins against the Lord, who
can intercede?' But Eli's sons wouldn't listen to their father, for the Lord was
already planning to put them to death."*

At this point we gain a new understanding concerning life in Christ.
Grasp this picture: the worship ascending from Israel initiated by Eli and
his two sons was carnal and fleshly even though Samuel was dwelling in
Israel. In the same way, as new believers, although Christ is living in us,
yet we may still be dominated by our flesh and the fruits (attitudes) of the
flesh may still be influencing the worship we give to God.

Romans 12:2 – *"Don't copy the behavior and customs of this world, but
let God transform you into a new person by changing the way you think.
Then you will know what God wants you to do, and you will know how
good and pleasing and perfect his will really is."* (NLT)

By virtue of our exposure to the secular media and our godless educational
system, the fact is: we are already conformed to this world in greater
proportion than we know. Our greatest need is to be transformed in our
thinking and the vehicle for that change is God's Word.

So, God lovingly teaches us by contrast because we are a fallen creation:
God's way verses my way, light vs. darkness, truth vs. the lie, etc. Obviously,
God's ways are different from man's ways; in fact, God's ways are so
different that I cannot learn them through simple trial and error methods.
Instead, I must learn God's ways from the instruction of God's Word and
by the revelation of the Holy Spirit.

So, let's look into God's Word and discover His will regarding acceptable
worship.

John 4:23-24 – *"But the time is coming and is already here, when* **by the power of God's Spirit** *people will worship the Father as he really is, offering him the true worship that he wants. God is Spirit, and only by the power of his Spirit can people worship him as he really is."* (TEV)

1 Peter 2:5 – *"And now you are living stones that are being used to build a spiritual house. You are also a group of holy* **priests***, and with the help of Jesus Christ you will* **offer sacrifices** *that please God."* (CEV)

Hebrews 13:15 – *"Let's take our place outside with Jesus, no longer pouring out the sacrificial blood of animals but pouring out* **sacrificial praises** *from our lips to God in Jesus' name."* (Msg)

Phil. 3:3 – *"For we are the circumcision, who* **worship God in the Spirit***, rejoice in Christ Jesus, and have no confidence in the flesh."* (NKJV)

Heb. 12:28-29 – *"We have been given possession of an unshakeable kingdom. Let us therefore* **be grateful** *and use our gratitude to* **worship God in the way that pleases him***, in reverence and fear. For our God is a consuming fire."* (NJB)

The worship that God declares "**acceptable**" is worship that originates out of our spirit, rather than from our soul. The prophets have pointed out that God cannot be properly worshiped by simply following some religious liturgy, whether that liturgy is 1,000 years old or initiated as recently as yesterday.

Psalm 50:12-15 – *"If I were hungry, I would not mention it to you, for all the world is mine and everything in it. I don't need the bulls you sacrifice; I don't need the blood of goats. What I want instead is your* **true thanks to God***; I want you to* **fulfill your vows** *to the Most High.* **Trust me** *in your times of trouble, and I will rescue you, and you will give me glory."*

Heb. 13:15 – *"With Jesus' help, let us continually offer our* **sacrifice of praise** *to God by proclaiming the glory of his name."*

God wants our worship to be offered in Spirit and Truth. That means we are attributing worth to God, in the marvel of His works and the majesty of His person, and we are doing it the way His Word instructs us to worship, with our whole heart and from a clear conscience. Any other kind of worship is not acceptable to God.

Isa. 29:13 – *"… this people draw near Me with their mouth and honor Me with their lips but remove their hearts and minds far from Me, and their fear and reverence for Me are a commandment of men that is learned by repetition [without any thought as to the meaning]."* (Amp)

God has one intention as our heavenly Father – to redeem us from our fallen state and share His very life, character and nature with us, so we can all enjoy fellowship together forever.

Vs. 12 – *"Now the sons of Eli were corrupt; they did not know the Lord."* (NLT)

The flesh always wars against the Spirit and thus is totally contrary to God's will and ignorant of God's ways. So, when we worship, while being influenced by the works of the flesh (Hophni and Phinehas), we fail to serve the Lord or His people; we simply gravitate to serving our own selfish desires.

How many of us, at one time or another, have gone to church to **get** blessed, rather than to **give** by seeking to be a blessing to God and others?

When God gave the sacrifices and offerings to Israel, in each case, He claimed the **fat** (what God has marked for destruction) for Himself and required that it be consumed by fire. The fat represents the carnal efforts of man in his attempt to please God.

The very act of worshiping God in a way that satisfies us, rather than offering to God what He requires, is synonymous with failing to consume the fat.

Lev. 17:5-6 – *"The meaning of this command is that the people of Israel shall now bring to the Lord the animals which they used to kill in the open country. They shall now bring them to the priest at the entrance of the Tent and kill them as fellowship offerings. The priest shall throw the blood against the sides of the altar at the entrance of the Tent and **burn the fat** to produce an odor that is pleasing to the Lord."* (TEV)

Many Christians think that going it alone and independently worshiping God in nature's surroundings, instead of gathering with the saints at God's designated place of worship, is pleasing to God. But what used to be overlooked by God, because of our ignorance, is no longer acceptable to Him. Now we must worship the way it pleases our heavenly Father.

Lev. 3:14-17 – *"Part of this offering must be presented to the Lord as an offering made by fire. This part includes the fat around the internal organs… The priest will burn them on the altar… an offering made by fire… Remember, **all the fat belongs to the Lord**…."* (NLT)

Leviticus 7:23-25 *"Give the Israelites these instructions: **You must never eat fat**, whether from oxen or sheep or goats… Anyone who eats fat from an offering given to the Lord by fire must be cut off from the community."*

There are two key phrases from these next two verses that help us understand how the fruits of the flesh (Hophni and Phinehas) influence our worship.

1 Sam. 2:13-14 – *"…with a fleshhook of three teeth in his hand…the priest took for himself."* (NLT)

The fat was consecrated to the Lord and was to be consumed by fire before the Lord. But, when we take what God provides and simply consume it upon ourselves, instead of acknowledging that all praise, honor, glory, and power belongs to God, we end up thinking we don't need God anymore.

Deut. 32:15 – *"Israel, you grew fat and rebelled against God, your Creator; you rejected the Mighty Rock, your only place of safety."* (CEV)

Amazingly, there are three primary sins that trip up secular and spiritual leaders today: Lust, Money, and Power (fame).

1 Sam. 2:15-16 – *"…**before** they burnt (consumed) the fat."* (NLT)

Before God receives what belongs to Him, the flesh takes for itself. If, instead of giving God the glory, giving God the praise, giving God the honor, we only sing what pleases us and only pray for what benefits us; the result of our flesh's influence on worship will be that people will learn to abhor the Lord's offering.

Hosea 8:12-13 – *"I have written many teachings for them, but they think the teachings are strange and foreign. The Israelites offer sacrifices to me as gifts and eat the meat, but the Lord is not pleased with them. He remembers the evil they have done, and he will punish them for their sins. They will be slaves again as they were in Egypt."* (NCV)

When we offer half-hearted worship and praise to God, by failing to put our whole heart into rejoicing in the God of our salvation, we simply end up exalting religious tradition, which makes the Word of God ineffectual in our lives. We simply slide back into bondage and slavery to our own fleshly desires.

Are we seeking to please ourselves, or are we seeking to please the Lord?

I ask this question to help us consider and evaluate our obedience to the Lord in giving Him the kind of worship that He requires.

Psalm 95:1 – *"Come, let us **sing for joy** to the Lord; let us **shout aloud** to the Rock of our salvation."* (NIV)

Col. 3:16 – *"Let the word of Christ dwell in you richly as you teach and admonish one another with all wisdom, and as you **sing psalms, hymns and spiritual songs** with gratitude in your hearts to God."* (NIV)

II. Eli's Fleshly Rebuke For the Sins of His Sons

To **Admonish** (*noutheteō*) means literally "to put in mind," with the purpose of warning and reproving. It presupposes that something is wrong and its intention is to correct, to make right. Its purpose is to bring about a change—in belief, attitude, habit, lifestyle, or in whatever way is needed. In fact, it is a warning to change or incur judgment.

One of the requirements for spiritual leadership in the New Testament states: *"He must manage his own family well, having children who respect and obey him. For if a man cannot manage his own household, how can he take care of God's church?"* (1 Tim. 3:4-5)

Eli was a spiritual leader who functioned as high priest at the tabernacle in Shiloh; he was also an irresponsible father. Eli really needed God's instruction from Proverbs on how to raise and discipline his sons, but regrettably, his sons were well beyond the conversation stage.

Now, what many believers don't realize is that the flesh cannot produce spiritual change. Flesh can only reproduce flesh and only the Spirit of Christ can produce spiritual, godly change. So when we try to discipline our children in the energy of our flesh (from anger or bitterness or resentment or out of frustration), instead of in the spirit of Christ, we only produce a fleshly reaction in our children and they are not graced to do God's will and truly obey from the heart.

Rather than disciplining his sons when they were young, he endeavored to admonish them in their adulthood when they were already beyond his control.

Their sinful behavior in manipulating the sacrificial offerings to serve their own lustful purposes was not their only transgression. They were also committing fornication with the young women who assisted in the sacrificial worship at the tabernacle.

Nearly blind, Eli became isolated and disengaged from the kind of worship taking place in the tabernacle, and thus, he only became aware of his son's transgressions when the people informed him.

When at last he took action to rebuke them, they refused to listen to the voice of their father, rejecting the authority God had placed over them.

What we need to learn from this passage is that our sin nature does not have the capacity to control or curtail sinful behavior. Rather, flesh reproduces flesh. The apostle Paul teaches us that when we endeavor with the strength of our will to curtail the appetites of the flesh, we will surely fail.

Rom. 7:13b – 20 – *"So we can see how terrible sin really is. It uses God's good commands for its own evil purposes. So the trouble is not with the law, for it is spiritual and good. The trouble is with me, for I am all too human, a slave to sin. I don't really understand myself, for I want to do what is right, but I don't do it. Instead, I do what I hate. But if I know that what I am doing is wrong, this shows that I agree that the law is good. So I am not the one doing wrong; it is sin living in me that does it. And I know that nothing good lives in me, that is, in my sinful nature. I want to do what is right, but I can't. I want to do what is good, but I don't. I don't want to do what is wrong, but I do it anyway. But if I do what I don't want to do, I am not really the one doing wrong; it is sin living in me that does it."*

There is only one solution for the sin nature we all received from Adam, and God gives us His sentence in 1 Sam. 2:25, *"for it was the will of the Lord to put them to death."*

God has placed the sentence of death on the sin nature. There is no redemption for your sin nature. Your sin nature will never be perfected and it will never get into heaven. That's why it is appointed unto man to die. We die to totally put off the sin nature, which dwells in our physical bodies. In the resurrection, we receive a new body, free from a sin nature; it will be like the Lord's resurrection body (1 Cor. 15:48-57).

People think that when a person gets saved by believing on the Lord Jesus Christ, the sin nature gets converted and you become a better person. Actually, your sin nature is not getting better or being reformed, rather the spiritual growth that a Christian experiences is really the process of learning how to receive God's grace by drawing upon the life of Christ.

It is learning to draw upon His life that enables you to obey the Holy Spirit's promptings and live in victory over the sin nature, free from having to commit the sinful acts prompted by our sin nature.

1 Sam 2:18, 21, 26 – Samuel dwelling in Israel is a type of Christ dwelling in the believer and the maturing of the believer is simply the increase of Christ in your life.

Rom. 8:6-8 – *"If your sinful nature controls your mind, there is death. But if the Holy Spirit controls your mind, there is life and peace. For the sinful nature is always hostile to God. It never did obey God's laws, and it never will. That's why those who are still under the control of their sinful nature can never please God."* (NLT)

One thing we can learn from this passage is that as a new believer in Christ, our flesh can still dominate us in various areas of our life. This level of spiritual maturity is described by the apostle Paul as being a "carnal Christian" (1 Cor. 3:3).

However, God loves us and has made provision to free us from the domination of our own flesh. In order to free us, the first thing God does is to send His Word, which exposes our sinful attitudes and sinful behavior.

III. God's Pronouncement of Judgment on Eli's House

Rev. 3:19 – *"Those whom I love I **rebuke** and **discipline**. So be earnest, and repent."* (NIV)

When there is something wrong in our lives – we're either missing the mark, allowing immoral or unclean thoughts to find lodging in our heads, or actually walking in sinful behavior – the first thing God does is to convict us by the Holy Spirit, and confront us through His holy Scriptures, then He sends His messengers.

Often, God uses people with a prophetic gifting, individuals specifically called and anointed to deliver His message to people, but the reality is He can use anyone, even a donkey, as in the case of Balaam (<u>Num. 22:28-32</u>).

John 1:6 – *"There was a man sent from God, whose name was John."* (KJV)

John was true to his prophetic anointing and confronted sinful behavior wherever he found it, calling people to repentance, so their hearts would be prepared for the coming of Messiah. Herod, however, did not respond properly to the rebuke of the Lord.

Luke 3:19-20 – *"But Herod, the ruler, stung by **John's rebuke** in the matter of Herodias, his brother Philip's wife, capped his long string of evil deeds with this outrage: He put John in jail."* (Msg)

All of God's ministers have been called to take His message to the ends of the earth, and, in the process, they are responsible to correct, rebuke, and encourage the people.

I don't think anyone enjoys being rebuked by a fellow believer and yet that's just as legitimate a function of ministry, as is encouragement.

2 Tim. 4:1-2 – *"And so I solemnly urge you before God and before Christ Jesus—who will someday judge the living and the dead when he appears to set up his Kingdom: Preach the word of God. Be persistent, whether the time is favorable or not. Patiently **correct**, **rebuke**, and **encourage** your people with good teaching."*

Looking at our text, we see that God, in great mercy and faithfulness, sends His messenger to rebuke the disobedient and sinful behavior of Eli. The Almighty is a God of judgment and He has made a decision about what needs to happen in Israel. So the man of God pronounced to Eli the judgment of the Lord. God wants change in Israel, so He's intervening to make sure change happens.

1 Sam. 2:27-28 – *"Then **a man of God came to Eli** and said to him, 'Thus says the LORD: **Did I not clearly reveal Myself** to the house of your father **when they were in Egypt** in Pharaoh's house? Did I not **choose** him out of all the tribes of Israel **to be My priest**, to offer upon My altar, to burn incense, and to wear an ephod before Me? And did I not give to the house of your father all the offerings of the children of Israel made by fire?"* (NKJV)

God not only revealed Himself to all of Israel while they were still in bondage in Egypt, but He specifically revealed Himself to Aaron's household and chose them to serve in priestly ministry in His dwelling place. What a privilege!

To be chosen by God is not a light thing. To be given a specific role in God's kingdom that calls for specific responsibilities to be fulfilled (sacrifices and offerings), that's no small thing.

Today, under the New Covenant, we are also specifically called and chosen by God to be a royal priesthood and to offer spiritual sacrifices by Jesus Christ that truly please God. (1 Peter 2:5, 9)

IV. What's All the Kicking About?

I Sam. 2:29 – *"Why do you **kick** at My sacrifice and My offering, which I have **commanded** in My **dwelling place**...?"* (NKJV)

Have you ever seen a child lying on the floor of a supermarket or department store, **kicking** and crying uncontrollably? What's that called? Yes, a temper tantrum! What is the child doing through this audio/visual display? The child is **resisting the will of the parent,** who in all probability just told the child they could not have another toy, a candy bar, or the latest game for his XBOX. In essence, the child is honoring their personal desires over the commandment of the parent.

However, in this case, Eli, the parent is honoring his kids over the commandment of God. That's known as child-centered parenting, which produces uncontrolled and self-willed children.

Like Eli, we think we are investing in the future of our children by putting them first. We think by making our children so important and catering to their every whim and desire we are helping them develop their personalities and gifts.

All too frequently, our kids become better at sacking the quarterback, sinking a 3-pointer, or hitting a baseball than they do at taking out the garbage, doing the dishes or learning how to fix a nutritious meal; let alone, knowing how to counter their teacher's promotion of godless ideologies like atheistic evolution, situational ethics, relativism, or the supposed value of false religions.

To "kick" means to resist, withstand, to rebel against, to despise or kick in scorn and Eli is not the only Biblical personality to learn about this kicking behavior as a method of resisting God's will.

Another well-known personality gives his personal testimony in the New Testament.

Acts 26:14 – *"We all fell to the ground, and I heard a voice saying to me in Aramaic, 'Saul, Saul, why do you persecute me? It is hard for you to **kick** against the **goads**.' "* (NIV)

Eccles. 12:11 – *"Words of wisdom are like the stick a farmer uses to make animals move. These sayings come from God, our only shepherd, and they are like nails that fasten things together."* (CEV)

God's words of wisdom, spoken by people like Stephen, were like a sharp stick, jabbing Saul in the heart, helping him see that Jesus is Lord.

Deut. 32:15 – *"Israel grew fat and **kicked**...they left the God who made them and rejected the Rock who saved them."* (NCV)

There can definitely be a down side to prosperity. Getting rich can make us feel that we don't need any outside help. Our flesh tries to convince us that the wealth we have accumulated was simply gained by our wise investments and hard work. What's the problem with that reasoning?

That kind of reasoning means we have forgotten that the only reason we were able to prosper was due to the blessing of God.

V. The Acceptable Sacrifice

<u>I Sam. 2:29</u> – *"Why do you kick at **My sacrifice** and **My offering**, which I have **commanded** in **My dwelling place**…? "* (NKJV)

God has given to every priest the responsibility of presenting "My sacrifice" and "My offering". In fact, He has **commanded** a specific sacrifice and offering in the place where He dwells.

I first began to understand what God desired from my life when He took me to the book of Romans. While reading the 12th chapter my eyes were opened to fresh truth.

<u>Romans 12:1</u> – *"Therefore, I urge you, brothers, in view of God's mercy, to offer your bodies as **living** sacrifices, **holy** and **pleasing** to God – this is your spiritual act of worship."* (NIV)

As I began to analyze this verse, I saw that God wants a living, holy, and acceptable sacrifice to be offered in His dwelling place. This is the highest form of worship I can offer God. Yet, how can I do that, when life, holiness, and acceptability does not originate with me? I'm just a sinner saved by grace.

- **"Living"** – (Greek) "Zoe." God's eternal life does not originate with me.

<u>1 John 5:11-12</u> – *"And this is what God has testified: He has given us eternal life, and this life is in his Son. So whoever has God's Son has life; whoever does not have his Son does not have life."* (NLT)

<u>John 5:39-40</u> – *"You search the Scriptures, because you think you will find eternal life in them. The Scriptures tell about me, but you refuse to come to me for eternal life."* (CEV)

- **"Holy"** – Jesus is the source of holiness.

FRANK R. DAVIS

Matthew 1:18 – *"Now this is how Jesus the Messiah was born. His mother, Mary, was engaged to be married to Joseph. But while she was still a virgin, she became pregnant by the Holy Spirit."* (NLT)

1 Cor. 1:30 – *"You are partners with Christ Jesus because of God. Jesus has become our wisdom sent from God, our righteousness, **our holiness**, and our ransom from sin."* (GW)

Hebrews 2:11 – *"So now Jesus and **the ones he makes holy** have the same Father."*

- **"Acceptable"** – Jesus alone is the pure, spotless, and acceptable sacrifice.

Eph. 1:6 – *"… He made us **accepted** in the Beloved."* (NKJV)

Hebrews 13:20-21 – *"The God of peace brought the great shepherd of the sheep, our Lord Jesus, back to life through the blood of an eternal promise. May this God of peace prepare you to do every good thing he wants. May he work in us **through Jesus Christ** to do what is pleasing to him. Glory belongs to Jesus Christ forever. Amen."* (GW)

Eph. 5:1-2 – *"You are God's children whom he loves, so try to be like him. Live a life of love just as Christ loved us and gave himself for us as a sweet-smelling offering and sacrifice to God."* (NCV)

So, the question comes to mind – since Jesus is the only "living, holy, acceptable sacrifice," what am I offering up to God on a daily basis? Do I offer the good works of Frank Davis or am I offering the expression of the nature of Jesus Christ, while doing the will of my heavenly Father?

1 Sam. 2:30 – *"Therefore the LORD God of Israel says: '**I said** indeed that your house and the house of your father would walk before Me forever.' **But now** the LORD says: 'Far be it from Me; for those who **honor Me** I will honor, and those who despise Me shall be lightly esteemed.'"* (NKJV)

Under the Old Covenant God made numerous promises to the children of Israel, one of which was this promise that Eli's house would walk before the Lord forever. However, because the flesh wars against the Spirit, the flesh would never come under and submit to God's holy Word.

Jesus describes this reality in His parable of the Ten Minas.

Luke 19:12-14 – *"Therefore He said: 'A certain nobleman went into a far country to receive for himself a kingdom and to return. So he called ten of his servants, delivered to them ten minas, and said to them, 'Do business till I come.' But his citizens hated him, and sent a message after him, saying, 'We will not have this man to reign over us.'"* (NKJV)

The flesh doesn't want the Word of God to rule in our lives and so it rejects God's Word being made flesh in us. Paul describes this struggle between the flesh and the Spirit in his epistle to the Romans. He also points out the means of victory to actually fulfilling the righteous demands of God's law.

Rom. 8:2-4 – *"For the power of the life-giving Spirit has freed you through Christ Jesus from the power of sin that leads to death. The law of Moses could not save us, because of our sinful nature. But God put into effect a different plan to save us. He sent his own Son in a human body like ours, except that ours are sinful. God destroyed sin's control over us by giving his Son as a sacrifice for our sins. He did this so that the requirement of the law would be fully accomplished for us who no longer follow our sinful nature but instead follow the Spirit."* (NLT)

Paul is saying that God's law-word taught us right from wrong, but even though we desired to obey the law and do what was right, our sin nature was stronger than our desire to obey and thus mankind has never been able to perfectly obey the law. But God's plan included a new covenant established through the sacrificial death of Jesus, which destroyed sin's power over us. Now, the writer to the Hebrews states it this way:

Hebrews 8:8-10, 13 – *"But God himself found fault with the old one when he said: 'The day will come, says the Lord, when I will make a new covenant with the people of Israel and Judah.*

This covenant will not be like the one I made with their ancestors when I took them by the hand and led them out of the land of Egypt. They did not remain faithful to my covenant, so I turned my back on them, says the Lord. But this is the new covenant I will make with the people of Israel on that day, says the Lord: I will put my laws in their minds so they will understand them, and I will write them on their hearts so they will obey them. I will be their God, and they will be my people.'

When God speaks of a new covenant, it means he has made the first one obsolete. It is now out of date and ready to be put aside." (NLT)

Here's what we need to see – every believer who enters into a covenant relationship with God, through faith in Jesus Christ, faces a time in their growth-process as a child of God, when the Lord will no longer allow Eli (the flesh) to rule in our hearts and taint or despise the sacrifice that God has commanded to be offered in His habitation.

The day comes when we are called into accountability for our lifestyle. We are responsible to honor Christ above everything in our lives. God loves us, but He is also committed to bringing us into fullness of life in Christ.

Notice Jesus' words in Luke's gospel.

Luke 14:26 – *"If you want to be my follower you must love me more than your own father and mother, wife and children, brothers and sisters—yes, more than your own life. Otherwise, you cannot be my disciple."*

Worship is not just singing on Sunday, or giving the tithe to God, or listening to the preaching of God's Word. Worship is a lifestyle! It is making Christ and His Word preeminent in all things: in our family, the way we relate to others, the way we do business, our educational process, our health choices, and in our play. God's will is for Jesus to become our very LIFE.

In the next chapter we will observe the faithful love of God promising to deal with the rebellious sin nature and raise up a **faithful priest** (Jesus Christ) in **Israel** (the believer) who will do all His will.

Galatians 2:20 – "My old self has been crucified with Christ. It is no longer I who live, but Christ lives in me. So I live in this earthly body by trusting in the Son of God, who loved me and gave himself for me." (NLT)

CHAPTER SEVEN

Understanding That God Keeps His Promises

I. The Promise of a Faithful Priest

<u>1 Sam. 2:31</u>– *"Behold, the days are coming that I will cut off your arm and the **arm** of your father's house, so that there will not be an old man in your house."* (NKJV)

Both the hand and the arm are Biblical images used to depict power or strength. These images depict a power used toward fulfilling a specific purpose, which may be either for good or evil.

For example, the Psalmist praises God, whose "arm is endued with power", but elsewhere he pleads with God to "break the arm of the wicked" who preys on the weak. (<u>Psa. 89:13</u>; <u>10:15</u>)

Moses describes God's "mighty hand and outstretched arm" as being synonymous "with great terror and with miraculous signs and wonders." (<u>Deut. 26:8</u>)

Jeremiah states that "by His great power and outstretched arm" the Lord created the heavens and the earth. (<u>Jer. 32:17</u>)

Isaiah describes God's holy arm as the means of providing salvation for all mankind.

Isaiah 52:10 – *"The Lord will lay bare his holy arm in the sight of all the nations, and all the ends of the earth will see the salvation of our God."* (NIV)

In the **literal** sense, God is rejecting Eli and his descendents as the ones to bear the priesthood responsibilities for Israel. This pronouncement of judgment was literally carried out under the leadership of Solomon in 1 Kings 2:27.

However, in the **figurative** sense, the Word of the Lord coming through the man of God is a promise that in the near future the arm or strength of the flesh will cease to dominate in Israel (the believer) and will ultimately be removed forever.

Why is this promise so important? It's important because without faith (the exercise of our personal capacity to believe and act upon what God says) it is impossible to please God. Believing and acting on this promise of Divine intervention is what actually frees us from trusting in the flesh and enables us to start trusting in the Lord.

Jeremiah 17:5-8 – *"This is what the Lord says: '**Cursed is the one who trusts in man**, who depends on **flesh for his strength** and whose heart turns away from the Lord. He will be like a bush in the wastelands; he will not see prosperity when it comes. He will dwell in the parched places of the desert, in a salt land where no one lives.*

*'But **blessed is the man who trusts in the Lord**, whose confidence is in him. He will be like a tree planted by the water that sends out its roots by the stream. It does not fear when heat comes; its leaves are always green. It has no worries in a year of drought and never fails to bear fruit.'"* (NIV)

2 Chron. 32:7-8 – *"'Be strong and courageous. Do not be afraid or discouraged because of the king of Assyria and the vast army with him, for there is a greater power with us than with him. With him is only **the arm of flesh**, but with us is the Lord our God to help us and to fight our battles.' And the people gained confidence from what Hezekiah the king of Judah said."* (NIV)

1 Peter 1:23-25 – *"For you have been born again. Your new life did not come from your earthly parents because the life they gave you will end in death. But **this new life** will last forever because it **comes from the***

*eternal, **living word of God**. As the prophet says, 'People are like grass that dies away; their beauty fades as quickly as the beauty of wildflowers. The grass withers, and the flowers fall away. But the word of the Lord will last forever....*" (NLT)

The nature we received from our parents is the "Adamic nature," which is under God's judgment and is destined to die; it cannot inherit the kingdom of God. However, the new life and nature we received from Christ, the Eternal Word of God, will last forever.

So, in order for a believer to cease the constant looking to the Adamic nature as a source of strength, he must, instead, have a clear revelation of his identification with Christ.

II. The Flesh Has an Enemy

As God's children, the New Testament scriptures inform us that we have three enemies: the world-system, the flesh, and the Devil. (1 John 2:15-17) (Gal. 5:19; 6:8) (1 Pet. 5:8)

Did you know that your flesh has an enemy? The Apostle Paul describes the conflict:

Gal. 5:17 – *"The old sinful nature loves to do evil, which is just opposite from what the Holy Spirit wants. And the Spirit gives us desires that are opposite from what the sinful nature desires. These two forces are constantly fighting each other, and your choices are never free from this conflict."* (NLT)

1 Sam. 2:32-33 – *"And you will **see** an enemy in My dwelling place, despite all the good, which God does for Israel. And there shall not be an old man in your house forever. But any of your men whom I do not cut off from My altar shall consume your eyes and grieve your heart. And all the descendants of your house shall die in the flower of their age."* (NKJV)

1 Sam. 2:32-33 – *"You will **watch** with envy as I pour out prosperity on the people of Israel. But no members of your family will ever live out their days. Those who are left alive will live in sadness and grief, and their children will die a violent death."* (NLT)

What God is promising us here is to bless Israel (the believer) in spite of the fact that Eli's descendents are continually trying to rear their ugly heads. The flesh will truly envy the spiritual prosperity of Israel (the believer) and will continually war with the Spirit to try to get back into a place of ruling and reigning over the believer.

But God promises to intervene and deal with every one of the fruits of the flesh that tries to manifest and then dominate in the life of the believer and He promises that their manifestation will be short-lived.

III. The Signs Point to a Fulfilled Promise

1 Sam. 2:34 – *"Now this shall be a **sign** to you that will come upon your two sons, on Hophni and Phinehas: in one day they shall die, both of them."* (NKJV)

It is very interesting to me that throughout the Bible, God continually gives signs to His covenant people. When **Abraham** believed God's promise of future descendents, and yet couldn't quite believe that the land of Israel would be given to him; he asked, "How can I be sure that you will give it to me?" Then God gave him the sign of covenant. (Gen. 15:8)

When **Moses** was being sent to deliver Israel from Egypt, he said, "What if they do not believe me or listen to me…;" so, God gave Moses three miraculous signs to demonstrate that God had sent him. (Ex. 4:1)

When the angel of the Lord challenged **Gideon** to deliver Israel from Midian oppression, Gideon replied, "If now I have found favor in your eyes, give me a sign that it is really you talking to me." So, God gave Gideon the sign of the fleece to help him believe. (Judges 6:17)

When the angel Gabriel told **Zechariah**, John the Baptist's father, that he would have a son, Zechariah said to the angel, "How can I know this will happen?" So, God gave him a sign and the angel said, "Since you didn't believe what I said, you won't be able to speak until the child is born." (Luke 1:18)

Isaiah 7:10-14 – *"Not long after this, the Lord sent this message to King Ahaz: 'Ask me for a sign, Ahaz, to prove that I will crush your enemies as I have* *promised. Ask for anything you like, and make it as difficult as you want.' But the king refused. 'No,' he said, 'I wouldn't test the Lord like that.'*

*Then Isaiah said, 'Listen well, you royal family of David! You aren't satisfied to exhaust my patience. You exhaust the patience of God as well! All right then, **the Lord himself will choose the sign**. Look! The virgin will conceive a child! She will give birth to a son and will call him Immanuel—'God is with us.'"*

<u>**Matthew 16:4**</u> – *"You want a **sign** because you are evil and won't believe! But the only sign you will be given is what happened to Jonah. Then Jesus left."* (CEV)

When you read the gospel of John you come to understand that John chose 7 miraculous signs performed by Jesus, **1)** Turning the water into wine; **2)** The healing of the Nobleman's son; **3)** Healing the lame man at the pool; **4)** The feeding of the five thousand; **5)** Walking on the water; **6)** Healing the man born blind; and **7)** Raising Lazarus from the dead.

Why? *"...so **that you may believe** that Jesus is the Messiah, the Son of God, and that by believing in him you will have life."* (<u>John 20:31</u>)

In an amazing display of mercy, God gives an unbelieving generation a sign. A sign is given for two reasons: **first**, to assist us in believing He will actually fulfill His promises to us and **second**, to hold us accountable for either choosing or rejecting the truth. What a gracious God!

IV. Christ The Faithful Priest – He Fulfills God's Promise

God's promise was to dethrone Eli from ruling in Israel (the believer) and raise up Samuel (type of Christ), a faithful priest, to take his place as the one to offer a pleasing sacrifice up to God.

<u>**1 Sam. 2:35**</u> – *"Then I will raise up for Myself a **faithful priest** who shall do according to what is in My heart and in My mind."* (NKJV)

Historically, for the nation of Israel, this passage in 1 Samuel was fulfilled when the priesthood was taken from Abiathar, descendant of Aaron's son Ithamar, and given to Zadok, descendant of Aaron's son Eleazar.

1 Kings 2:27 – *"So Solomon removed Abiathar from the priesthood of the Lord, fulfilling the word the Lord had spoken at Shiloh about the house of Eli."* (NIV)

But in the ultimate sense the "faithful Priest" and "Anointed One" are one and the same, the Lord Jesus Christ. He is both Priest and King (Psa. 110; Heb. 5:6; Rev. 19:16).

The immediate fulfillment of God's promise, to replace Eli with a faithful priest, is Samuel; however, it is also very clear that Samuel is a type of Christ, the ultimate faithful High Priest.

Hebrews 2:17 – *"Therefore, it was necessary for Jesus to be in every respect like us, his brothers and sisters, so that he could be our merciful and faithful High Priest before God. He then could offer a sacrifice that would take away the sins of the people."*

Rev. 19:11-13 – *"Then I saw heaven opened, and a white horse was standing there. And the one sitting on the horse was named **Faithful and True**. For he judges fairly and then goes to war. His eyes were bright like flames of fire, and on his head were many crowns. A name was written on him, and only he knew what it meant. He was clothed with a robe dipped in blood, and his title was **the Word** of God."*

V. As the Faithful Priest, He Receives an Established House

1 Sam. 2:35 – *"I will build him a **sure house**, and he shall walk before My anointed forever."* (NKJV)

1 Sam. 2:35 – *"I will give him descendants, who will always serve in the presence of my chosen king."* (TEV)

In the New Testament we see that Jesus is not only the faithful High Priest, he is also the Lord in charge of God's house.

Hebrews 3:1-6 – *"My Christian friends, who also have been called by God! Think of **Jesus**, whom God sent to be **the High Priest** of the faith we profess. He was faithful to God, who chose him to do this work, just as Moses was faithful in his work in God's house. A man who builds a house receives more* *honor than the house itself. In the same way Jesus is worthy of much greater honor than Moses. Every house, of course, is built by someone—and God is the one who has built all things. Moses was faithful in God's house as a servant, and he spoke of the things that God would say in the future. But Christ is faithful as the Son in charge of God's house.* **We are his house** *if we keep up our courage and our confidence in what we hope for."* (TEV)

Hebrews 10:21 – *"We have a superior priest in charge of God's house."* (GW)

1 Peter 2:5 – *"And now you are living stones that are being used to build a spiritual house. You are also a group of holy priests, and with the help of Jesus Christ you will offer sacrifices that please God."* (CEV)

VI. The Flesh Longs to Experience Spiritual Life – But Can't!

1 Sam. 2:36 – *"And it shall come to pass that everyone who is left in your house will come and* **bow down** *to him for a piece of* **silver** *and a* **morsel of bread***, and say, 'Please, put me in one of the priestly positions, that I may eat a piece of bread.' "* (NKJV)

To **bow** means to submit or to yield, to cease from competition or resistance.

Phil. 2:9-11 – *"Therefore God exalted him to the highest place and gave him the name that is above every name, that at the name of Jesus every knee should bow, in heaven and on earth and under the earth, and every tongue confess that Jesus Christ is Lord, to the glory of God the Father."* (NIV)

James 4:10 – *"When you bow down before the Lord and admit your dependence on him, he will lift you up and give you honor."* (NLT)

Our Adamic nature has to acknowledge the Lordship of the new nature from Christ and thus bows down, but it also wants to be accepted in its fallen state. That of course is impossible because God has already passed judgment on the flesh, "it shall not inherit the kingdom of God."

1 Cor. 6:9-10 – *"Don't you know that those who do wrong will have no share in the Kingdom of God? Don't fool yourselves. Those who indulge in* *sexual sin, who are idol worshipers, adulterers, male prostitutes, homosexuals, thieves, greedy people, drunkards, abusers, and swindlers—none of these will have a share in the Kingdom of God."* (NLT)

Paul, speaking of his Adamic fallen nature, tells us:

Romans 7:18 – *"I know I am rotten through and through so far as my old sinful nature is concerned. No matter which way I turn, I can't make myself do right. I want to, but I can't."* (NLT)

1 Cor. 15:50 – *"I declare to you, brothers, that flesh and blood cannot inherit the kingdom of God, nor does the perishable inherit the imperishable."* (NIV)

Paul goes on to say:

Romans 7:23, 25 – *"But I see another law working in my body, which makes war against the law that my mind accepts. That other law working in my body is the law of sin, and it makes me its prisoner. I thank God for saving me through Jesus Christ our Lord! So in my mind I am a slave to God's law, but in my sinful self I am a slave to the law of sin."* (NCV)

So, we see the conflict in Israel (believer), – our new nature (Samuel) is yielding to the Holy Spirit and our old sinful Adamic nature (Eli) is resisting the Holy Spirit.

The question then arises, "Which nature will we identify with or side with?"

When we identify with and rely on our old sinful self, we feel we don't need God's help and we put our trust in the arm of the flesh. We trust in our human rationale and rely on our worldly education to know what is right and what is wrong.

We even think our ways are better than God's ways. In fact, the deceptiveness of our sin nature tries to get us to believe we can become spiritually acceptable to God by redeeming ourselves through good works and religious activities.

The problem is that God has already passed judgment on the flesh – it will never be redeemed, it can never enter God's eternal kingdom.

Israel's experience, at this juncture, is equivalent to Paul's experience as described in Romans chapter 7. It is the war between the flesh and the Spirit of God. Here, in 1st Samuel, Israel (the believer) is receiving the promise from God that the flesh (Eli) and the fruits of the flesh (Hophni and Phinehas) will be dealt with by God's intervention.

Change is on the horizon for Israel. God is going to raise-up a new priest who will faithfully offer an acceptable sacrifice in God's habitation.

Now we know that the flesh nature must bow in submission to the new life we have in Christ, but as long as we are still in our earthly bodies, the flesh will beg for a little **silver** (redemption) and **bread** (spiritual food) and some kind of position of recognition. It wants to look legitimate to the rest of the world.

Like Paul, moving from Romans chapter 7 to chapter 8, we need to identify with our new nature – yielding to and depending upon the Holy Spirit to lead us into all truth.

When we look to the Holy Spirit, He uses God's Word to renew our mind and change the way we think so that we begin to see from God's perspective and then His grace actually empowers us to do God's will.

Jesus is the faithful priest that God has supernaturally placed in each believer. He alone can offer up an acceptable sacrifice to God. My encouragement to you is to get your eyes off of yourself and start "looking unto Jesus, the author and finisher of your faith."

<u>Gal. 2:20</u> – *"My old self has been crucified with Christ. It is no longer I who live, but Christ lives in me. So I live in this earthly body by trusting in the Son of God, who loved me and gave himself for me."*

If you find yourself constantly identifying with your old nature and struggling with one of the fruits of the flesh that has raised its ugly head in your life, don't despair; just start crying out for a fresh revelation of Jesus. He is the Savior who is able to save to the uttermost and He loves us more than we can fully comprehend!

CHAPTER EIGHT

The Importance of Hearing God's Voice

So far we have seen Israel, prior to Samuel's birth, as a religious person, Jew or Gentile; barren, and being provoked by a fruitful person (Peninnah). We observe Hannah praying without success until, finally, God's will was revealed to her and once she prayed according to the will of God, God heard her prayer and then God opened her womb.

The birth of Samuel speaks of the new birth of a believer, and Hannah's rejoicing is a type of the rejoicing in God that every believer should experience as they rejoice in God's great salvation.

However, Eli continued to rule and reign in Israel until the time appointed by God. Refusing to allow the sins of Hophni and Phinehas to continue, God sent His messenger to pronounce His judgment on Eli's house and to give the promise that He would raise up a faithful priest who would do all that was in God's heart and mind. In addition, God promised to build His faithful priest a sure house that would minister before His anointed forever.

This brings us to the spiritual condition of Israel as stated in the first four verses of chapter three. Israel (the believer) is growing in Christ, yet still ruled and motivated by Eli (the flesh) and still manifesting the fruits of the flesh (Hophni and Phinehas); Israel is indeed struggling spiritually and in need of a revelation of the Lordship of Christ.

1 Sam. 3:1-4a – *"Now the boy Samuel ministered to the Lord before Eli. And the word of the Lord was rare in those days; there was no widespread revelation. And it came to pass at that time, while Eli was lying down in* *his place, and when his eyes had begun to grow so dim that he could not see, and before the lamp of God went out in the tabernacle of the Lord where the ark of God was, and while Samuel was lying down, that the Lord called Samuel."* (NLT)

Have you ever wondered why God allowed David to serve so many years under Saul?

1 Samuel 18:1-2 – *"After David had finished talking with Saul, he met Jonathan, the king's son. There was an immediate bond of love between them, and they became the best of friends. From that day on Saul kept David with him at the palace and wouldn't let him return home."*

God had already rejected Saul from being the King over Israel, yet He allowed him to remain in office so that David could be trained for the job.

I have learned both through observation and through personal experience while serving as an associate pastor that God wants you to learn from every authority He places over you. There will be two things that you will learn from that authority: "How to do it" and "How not to do it."

Children, being under the authority of their parents, are in a position to learn either positive or negative traits from their parents. Parents actually make mistakes; and when that happens, children can learn to avoid making the same mistakes.

Each one of us could share examples of parents who have suffered with addictions and children who never want to put themselves in harm's way by embracing the same addiction.

On the other hand, we also know of children who have actually followed in their parent's footsteps by becoming, say an alcoholic, and suffering similar lifestyle consequences.

God, the Father, will place you under both good leaders and bad leaders in order to teach you what you need to learn in order to do His will. The highest goal in any situation is that we learn from the successes, as well as the mistakes of others, and seek to avoid the pain and suffering that accompanies sinful behavior.

I. The Scarcity of God's Word

<u>**1 Sam. 3:1-2a**</u> – *"And the word of the LORD was **rare** in those days... **Eli was lying down** in his place."* (NLT)

<u>**Amos 8:11-12**</u> – *"'The time is surely coming,' says the Sovereign Lord, 'when I will send a famine on the land—not a famine of bread or water but of hearing the words of the Lord. People will stagger everywhere from sea to sea, searching for the word of the Lord, running here and going there, but they will not find it.'"* (NLT)

Ever been in a situation like that? Longing to hear God's living Word to your heart and not hearing it. Running to this special meeting and then to that one, but no success. Maybe your search was limited to reading several books, but whatever the case, the answers you sought from God were not forth coming.

Have you learned that the flesh could care less if there is a scarcity of God's Word? The New King James Version describes Eli as "lying down." The flesh is always passive and careless when it comes to the Word of the Lord.

Do you find yourself too busy to have your daily devotions of Bible reading and prayer?

Do you have opportunities for small group Bible Study and yet, you don't take advantage of those opportunities?

The pastoral question I want to ask you is "Have you allowed your flesh to find alternative activities that result in making the Word of God a scarcity in your life?"

II. No Vision Producing Revelation of God

<u>**1 Sam. 3:1**</u>– *"And the word of the LORD was **rare** in those days; there was **no widespread revelation**."*

<u>**Prov. 29:18a**</u> – *"Where there is **no vision** [no redemptive revelation of God], the people (cast off restraint and) perish...."* (Amp.)

Life is a journey, and as you know, every journey has a destination. Everybody ends up somewhere.

Vision is what enables you to look beyond what is and paint a picture of what could be.

Clarity of vision stimulates the emotions and provides us with motivation, which enables us to endure the struggle of reaching our goal, such as, making the team, losing a specific amount of weight, obtaining a high school diploma or earning a college degree.

A clear vision dramatically increases your chances of coming to the end of your life, experiencing a deep sense of satisfaction, and reflecting on a life lived with God's purpose in mind, while fulfilling your destiny. You can testify, "I finished well. I kept the faith. My life counted for God."

Obviously, a great deal could be said about vision; however, it is the redemptive revelation of God that is lacking in this believer's life.

What I have learned over the years is that without this ongoing revelation of God's character and His will for our lives, every one of us would cast off restraint, disregarding God's Word and end up pursuing the sinful pleasures of the world-system, just like Hophni and Phinehas.

III. The Limitations of the Flesh

1 Sam. 3:2a – *"And it came to pass **at that time**, while Eli was lying down in his place..."*

1. Eli (The Flesh) can't see God's glorious purposes.

It is only pride and arrogance that makes us think we can see, when in reality, we can't. Our fleshly rationale is truly blind to the truth. Faith is the only path to understanding and knowing the truth. Paul describes our journey as being "from faith to faith."

Solomon, under the inspiration of the Holy Spirit says:

Proverbs 4:18-19 – *"The way of the righteous is like the first gleam of dawn, which shines ever brighter until the full light of day. But the way* *of the wicked is like complete darkness. Those who follow it have no idea what they are stumbling over."* (NLT)

The Apostle John understands the truth and says:

1 John 1:7 – *"But if we walk in the light, as he is in the light, we have fellowship with one another, and the blood of Jesus, his Son, purifies us from all sin."* (NIV)

Eph. 1:17-18 – *"I keep asking that the God of our Lord Jesus Christ, the glorious Father, may give you the Spirit of wisdom and revelation, so that you may know him better. I pray also that the eyes of your heart may be enlightened in order that you may know the hope to which he has called you, the riches of his glorious inheritance in the saints."* (NIV)

Paul prayed for the church because he knew that without the Spirit of wisdom and revelation giving us the knowledge of Jesus, we could not grasp the glorious riches of our inheritance as stored up for us in Christ.

The flesh can't see, so we walk by **faith** (the living Word of God) and not by **sight** (human rationale).

2. The Lamp in the Tabernacle is about to go out.

1 Sam. 3:3a – *"... **before the lamp of God went out** in the tabernacle of the LORD...."* (NLT)

Whenever the Word of the Lord is scarce in our lives, the lamp will grow dim and begin to go out. We can only walk in the light God gives us. Step away from the light and we will stumble and fall in the darkness.

Psalm 119:105 – *"Your word is a lamp for my feet and a light for my path."*

John 9:5 – *"While I am in the world, I am the light of the world."* (NIV)

John 12:35-36 – *"Jesus answered, 'The light will be with you for only a little longer. Walk in the light while you can. Then you won't be caught walking blindly in the dark. Have faith in the light while it is with you, and you will be children of the light.'"* (CEV)

If we are abiding in Christ and His Word is abiding is us, we become an expression of Christ's light to the world around us.

Eph. 5:13-14 – *"But when the light shines on them, it becomes clear how evil these things are. And where your light shines, it will expose their evil deeds."*

There were two kinds of light in the Tabernacle. The **candelabra,** which provided light for the Holy Place, and the **Shekinah glory** located in the Holy of Holies, radiating from above the Ark of the Covenant.

The light from the candelabra represents the illumination of God's Word in the soul and the Shekinah glory represents the revelation of God in our spirit.

Since Eli is blind, he can't help to rectify the fact that the lamp is about to go out; however, Samuel (Christ) is resting in the Holy Place and is the only one capable of keeping the candelabrum burning. The light in the Holy Place is necessary to understanding and applying the Word of God to your life.

IV. Coming To Know The Voice of The Lord

1 Sam. 3:7 – *"Now Samuel **did not yet know** the LORD, nor was the word of the LORD yet revealed to him."*

My own personal struggle to know the voice of the Lord began with the promptings of the Holy Spirit urging me to function in the gift of interpretation. This experience came during a Sunday evening service while we were worshiping the Lord in song. During a pause between worship songs, a particular individual gave an utterance in tongues and immediately after that utterance came to an end, the Spirit of the Lord moved upon my heart to give the interpretation.

The Lord dropped a couple of phrases into my mind and then urged me to begin speaking those phrases.

However, that's when a major battle began to take place in my mind. Along with the promptings of the Holy Spirit, the enemy began speaking into my mind telling me that it wasn't really God prompting me, but rather it was simply my strong desire to be of service to God as a source of edification to my fellow believers.

This struggle in my mind was a deafening silence that seemed to last for many seconds. Then someone else gave the interpretation – using almost the exact wording that the Holy Spirit had given me.

At the conclusion of the interpretation, a prophetic utterance was given by one of the ministers from the platform that was specifically addressed to me. The Lord immediately addressed my fear by telling me "My son, the word you received did not simply arise out of your desire to be used of Me; but in fact, I will use you to declare My goodness and speak forth My word. Don't be afraid, but speak as I place my word in your heart."

At that prophetic word, I broke into tears of repentance knowing that I had missed allowing God to use me to bring edification to Christ's body. That gentle word from the Lord allowed me to more specifically understand how God would speak into my spirit and it encouraged me to begin yielding to the Lord as He began expressing the gifts of the Holy Spirit in my life.

Now, the situation for Israel is definitely dark and foreboding. Eli (the flesh) is ruling in Israel (the believer). The source of life and victory – the Word of God – is scarce and Israel is devoid of any redemptive revelation of God. Eli is almost completely blind and the lamp of God is about to go out in God's habitation. Yet, in the midst of this dismal situation, God speaks.

It's important to note that Samuel is resting in the Holy Place where the **candelabrum,** the **Table of Showbread**, and the **Altar of Incense** were located.

The Holy Place, where Samuel was lying down, is a type of the soul of man. It contains three pieces of furniture representing the intellect, the will and the emotions. There is also a spiritual growth progression represented by the priestly ministry and the furniture of the Tabernacle.

An **outer court Christian** is one who focuses primarily on the brazen altar, where a sacrifice is offered providing salvation and the forgiveness of man's sins. Going beyond the brazen altar and deeper into Christ, the believer priest arrives at the laver. There are those who focus on sanctification, on the washing at the laver, cleaning up the external aspects of our lives. Both are necessary for any priest to enter the Holy Place.

A **Holy Place Christian** is one who has experienced the joy of sins forgiven and the sanctifying work of the Holy Spirit in cleaning up their external behavior, and now is also learning to receive Holy Spirit illumination upon God's Word (the bread of life) and also learning to worship and minister to the Lord in intercession at the altar of incense (Psa. 100).

A **Holy of Holies Christian** is one who continues to experience what an Outer Court Christian experiences as well as what a Holy Place Christian experiences, but in addition is receiving an ongoing revelation of the character and nature of the Living God.

By God's grace, they are becoming partakers of the divine nature (2 Pet. 1:4).

Essentially, Samuel's repose in the Holy Place, indicates that the growth of Israel, the believer, had reached the time in the growth process where the life of Christ would begin to exercise a more dominate role. This would begin with the Word of the Lord being revealed.

I want to encourage you by reminding you that God uses the desert to make you thirsty and the pit to get you to look up. Don't despair when the heat of God's testing is turned up and your flesh begins to manifest; instead, fix your eyes on Jesus the author and finisher of your faith.

V. Your Servant Hears

The Scripture declares that truthful testimony is established in the mouth of two or three witnesses. So while understanding our weakness as humans, God in His mercy speaks again concerning the house of Eli and pronounces His final judgment.

Only this time the Word of the Lord does not come from an external source, but instead through the priestly ministry of Samuel. As Samuel is dwelling in Israel, so Christ is dwelling in the believer and now the Word of the Lord is coming through the Spirit of Christ dwelling in your human spirit.

1 Sam. 3:10-20 – *"Now the LORD came and stood and called as at other times, "Samuel! Samuel!" And Samuel answered, "Speak, for **Your servant hears**."*

*Then the LORD said to Samuel: '**Behold**, I will do something in Israel at which both ears of everyone who hears it will **tingle**. In that day I will perform against Eli all that I have spoken concerning his house, **from beginning to end**. For I have told him that I will **judge his house forever** for the iniquity which he knows, because his sons made themselves vile, and he did not restrain them. And therefore I have sworn to the house of Eli that **the iniquity** of Eli's house **shall not be atoned for** by sacrifice or offering **forever.'***

So Samuel lay down until morning and opened the doors of the house of the LORD. And Samuel was afraid to tell Eli the vision. Then Eli called Samuel and said, 'Samuel, my son!'

He answered, "Here I am."

And he said, 'What is the word that the LORD spoke to you? Please do not hide it from me. God do so to you, and more also, if you hide anything from me of all the things that He said to you.' Then Samuel told him everything, and hid nothing from him. And he said, 'It is the LORD. Let Him do what seems good to Him.'

*So Samuel grew, and the LORD was with him and **let none of his words fall** to the ground. And **all Israel** from Dan to Beersheba **knew** that Samuel had been established as a prophet of the LORD."* (NKJV)

And Samuel answered, *"Speak,* for **Your servant hears***."*

Reading through the Old Testament you discover that God spoke directly to people. He spoke to Adam and Eve, to Noah, Abraham, Moses, Samuel, Isaiah, Jeremiah and so many others. When God spoke to Noah, there were no Bibles, preachers or churches. It was just God and Noah.

Gen. 6:12-16 – *"God observed all this corruption in the world, and he saw violence and depravity everywhere. So God said to Noah, 'I have decided to destroy all living creatures, for the earth is filled with violence because of them. Yes, I will wipe them all from the face of the earth!*

Make a boat from resinous wood and seal it with tar, inside and out. Then construct decks and stalls throughout its interior. Make it 450 feet long, 75 feet wide, and 45 feet high. Construct an opening all the way around the boat, 18 inches below the roof. Then put three decks inside the boat— bottom, middle, and upper—and put a door in the side.'" (NLT)

After God specified exactly how to build the ark, He went on to give instructions regarding Noah's family, the animals, and the food.

In the same manner, the voice of the Lord gave direct commands and promises to all of His servants. When God spoke to Samuel, it was not some vague impression coming to him while he was lying on the floor in the Holy Place within the Tabernacle.

In the New Testament, we also see men and women with hearing ears receiving God's Word. In John 10, Jesus taught his disciples about hearing and knowing his voice.

John 10:3-5, 14, 16, 27 – *"The gatekeeper opens the gate for him, and the sheep hear his voice and come to him. He calls his own sheep by name and leads them out. After he has gathered his own flock, he walks ahead of them, and they follow him because they recognize his voice. They won't follow a stranger; they will run from him because they don't recognize his voice.*

I am the good shepherd; I know my own sheep, and they know me. I have other sheep, too, that are not in this sheepfold. I must bring them also, and they will listen to my voice; and there will be one flock with one shepherd. My sheep recognize my voice; I know them, and they follow me." (NLT)

According to God's Word, Christ's disciples are to know, hear, and obey His voice. Now, He didn't just speak to the twelve apostles; He spoke to ordinary people, such as the lame man lowered through the roof, and the man born blind, and to disciples like Mary, Martha, and Lazarus and to Jews, like Zacchaeus, and Gentiles, like the centurion.

Before His ascension, Jesus promised that the Holy Spirit would come to live within each believer and He would receive what Jesus continued to speak, and then tell us what Jesus says.

Even now, the Holy Spirit is receiving truth from Jesus concerning things to come in your life. That's why it is so important to develop and maintain communion with God.

The New Testament believer lives by hearing the Word of Christ and being empowered by the Holy Spirit to do God's will.

Over and over the Scriptures admonish us: "Today if you will hear his voice, harden not your hearts." And again: "he that hath an ear to hear, let him hear what the Spirit is saying to the churches." Heb. 3: 7-8; Rev. 2:17

God's Spirit is talking, and the question remains: Are we listening? Do we have hearing ears?

VI. Hearing Ears Bear Witness

1 Sam. 3:11 – *"Then the LORD said to Samuel: 'Behold, I will do something in Israel at which both ears of everyone who hears it will tingle."*

The word "**behold**" is not a mere interjection, but is really a verb, telling us to actually look and see, to fix your gaze upon it and observe and note attentively.

"Behold" seems to be used by the Holy Spirit, in the same way the Lord Jesus uses the words, "**Verily, verily**, I say unto you".

Tingle: to experience a sudden feeling of unexpected wonder—'to be surprised. To be in a state of surprise or astonishment, implying awe bordering on fear.

In other words, everyone with hearing ears that hears about this new thing God is about to do, will instantly bear witness that it is the truth, the living Word of God.

VII. What God Starts – He Completes

<u>Phil. 1:6</u> – *"being confident of this, that he who began a good work in you will carry it on to completion until the day of Christ Jesus."* (NIV)

How do we know that what God starts, He continues to completion?

<u>Num. 23:19</u> – *"God is not a man, that he should lie. He is not a human, that he should change his mind. Has he ever spoken and failed to act? Has he ever promised and not carried it through?"* (NLT)

In talking to God about Israel's request for meat to eat:

<u>Num. 11:21-23</u> – *"Moses said, 'There are 600,000 foot soldiers here with me, and yet you promise them meat for a whole month! Even if we butchered all our flocks and herds, would that satisfy them? Even if we caught all the fish in the sea, would that be enough?'*

Then the Lord said to Moses, 'Is there any limit to my power? Now you will see whether or not my word comes true!'" (NLT)

In fulfillment of His Word, the Lord sent a huge windstorm that blew enough quail to the place where they were encamped that the people not only had plenty, but so much that many gorged themselves and died.

<u>Jer. 1:12</u> – *"The Lord said to me, 'you have seen correctly, because I am watching to make sure my words come true.'"* (NCV)

Have you been feeding on God's Word sufficiently to believe that what He says, He will also do?

VIII. God's Judgment on Eli's House

<u>1 Sam. 3:14</u> – *"therefore I have sworn to the house of Eli that **the iniquity of Eli's house shall not be atoned for** by sacrifice or offering **forever**."*

When we talk about the flesh in this instance, we're not talking about the human body. What we are talking about is the **sin nature** that dwells within the human body. (<u>Rom. 7</u>)

Eli represents the sin nature, which prompts sinful acts in our lives. Now, God's judgment is on Eli's house and there is no redemption for the flesh. In other words, there is no personal sacrifice or offering we can give to God that will redeem, save, or improve the sin nature – ever.

In fact, when Jesus died on the cross he accomplished two things: **First**, he bore our sins and died paying the penalty for sins, justifying us before God. **Second**, he died to sin once and for all, and when he died, we died with him and when he rose from the dead, we rose with him to walk in newness of life, by the glory of the Father.

Thus, when we identify with our old Adamic sin nature, sin has dominion over us and prompts us to do sinful acts. But when we identify with our new nature in Christ, the Holy Spirit empowers us to walk in newness of life and God's character becomes the expression of our lives.

<u>Heb. 10:26-31</u> – *"If we deliberately keep on sinning after we have received the knowledge of the truth, no sacrifice for sins is left, but only a fearful expectation of judgment and of raging fire that will consume the enemies of God. Anyone who rejected the law of Moses died without mercy on the testimony of two or three witnesses. How much more severely do you think a man deserves to be punished who has trampled the Son of God under foot, who has treated as an unholy thing the blood of the covenant that sanctified him, and who has insulted the Spirit of grace? For we know him who said, 'It is mine to avenge; I will repay,' and again, 'The Lord will judge his people.' It is a dreadful thing to fall into the hands of the living God."* (NIV)

The Lord Jesus Christ is the Judge of all the earth and no one can openly reject God's grace and mercy through Christ, continue in sin and fail to repent and still expect to avoid God's chastening rod. You can't know the truth, disregard it, and then expect God to overlook your transgression. God has the authority and He will execute that authority.

Daniel was given a glimpse of that judgment day.

<u>Dan. 7:9-10</u> – *"As I looked, thrones were put in their places, and God, who has been alive forever, sat on his throne. His clothes were white like snow, and the hair on his head was white like wool. His throne was made from fire, and the wheels of his throne were blazing with fire. A river of fire was* *flowing from in front of him. Many thousands of angels were serving him, and millions of angels stood before him. Court was ready to begin, and the books were opened."* (NCV)

IX. The Word of the Lord Endures Forever

<u>1 Sam. 3:19-20</u> – *"So Samuel grew, and the LORD was with him and **let none of his words fall** to the ground. And **all Israel** from Dan to Beersheba **knew** that Samuel had been established as a prophet of the LORD."* (NLT)

<u>Luke 2:40,</u> <u>47,</u> <u>49-52</u> – *"There the child grew up healthy and strong. He was filled with wisdom beyond his years, and God placed his special favor upon him. And all who heard him were amazed at his understanding and his answers.*

His parents didn't know what to think. 'Son!' his mother said to him… 'your father and I have been frantic, searching for you everywhere.' 'But why did you need to search?' he asked. 'You should have known that I would be in my Father's house.' But they didn't understand what he meant. Then he returned to Nazareth with them and was obedient to them; and his mother stored all these things in her heart. So Jesus grew both in height and in wisdom, and he was loved by God and by all who knew him." (NLT)

God's Word is a "living" Word. It lives and abides forever, which means it is relevant for believers in the 21st century. In fact, we will be living by God's Word forever, throughout the ceaseless ages.

God's living Word of judgment on Eli's house came to Samuel and Samuel communicated it to Eli and then to all Israel. That judgment by God is a decree, not a conditional promise, and it will not be changed.

Throughout Scripture, God has made many conditional pronouncements, such as His Word to Nineveh, "forty days from now Nineveh will be destroyed." But when the people repented, God changed his mind and refrained from bringing the promised judgment.

God has made a promise to Israel, the believer, and He has confirmed that Word in the mouth of two witnesses. His promise is to deal with Eli, the rebellious sin nature – also known as "the flesh", and to deal with the fruits or works of the flesh, represented by the lives of Hophni and Phinehas.

The amazing thing is that everyone who has ears to hear, when they hear about this promise from God to deal with Eli's house, will bear witness that it is true.

In addition, God promises that when He begins, He will not stop until He has completed the job.

Phil. 1:6 – *"Being confident of this, that he who began a good work in you will carry it on to completion until the day of Christ Jesus."* (NIV)

The questions I have for you are: Have you heard the Holy Spirit speaking this promise of God to raise up a faithful priest in you who will accomplish all His holy will; and have you heard the promise that God is going to deal with your sin nature?

Are you aware that God has already passed judgment on your sin nature? God's decree is that your fallen, sinful, Adamic nature will NOT inherit the Kingdom of God!

I believe that for many of you, God's promise to deal with Eli and his house is the message of hope that you have been longing to hear. And the Spirit of Christ in you is, right now, proclaiming this message of faith into your spirit.

You may be struggling with one or more manifestations of sin in your life and up to this moment you have wondered if you will ever get free. I am telling you that this promise is for you and that Jesus is well able to set you free from whatever sin holds you in bondage.

As a disciple and follower of Christ, the Lord wants you to have a hearing ear and to bear witness to the veracity of His promise. My prayer is that you will rise up in faith, believe and rejoice in God's Word of life and coming freedom!

CHAPTER NINE

The Transforming Power of God's Word

Initially, Samuel did not recognize God's voice when He called him, but now, Samuel clearly recognizes God's voice and is coming to know the Lord as revealed by His Word. The only way we can know God intimately is through His Word.

When Moses asked to behold God's glory, which is the manifestation of His character and nature, God obliged Moses, but with certain stipulations.

Exodus 33:18-23 – *"He then said, 'Please show me your glory.' Yahweh said, 'I shall make all my goodness pass before you, and before you I shall pronounce the name Yahweh; and I am gracious to those to whom I am gracious and I take pity on those on whom I take pity. But my face', he said, 'you cannot see, for no human being can see me and survive.' Then Yahweh said, 'Here is a place near me. You will stand on the rock, and when my glory passes by, I shall put you in a cleft of the rock and shield you with my hand until I have gone past. Then I shall take my hand away and you will see my back; but my face will not be seen.'"* (NJB)

From this account we can see clearly that God's revelation of Himself to Moses can only happen within certain parameters. <u>First</u>, Moses must be standing on the rock (Christ Jesus); <u>second</u>, Moses must be placed **in** the cleft (the pierced side of Christ crucified) of the rock; and <u>third</u>, only a partial revelation took place under the Old Covenant. The full revelation is reserved for later.

John 1:14 – *"The Word became flesh and blood, and moved into the neighborhood. We saw the glory with our own eyes, the one-of-a-kind* *glory, like Father, like Son, Generous inside and out, true from start to finish."* (Msg)

2 Cor. 4:6 – *"The God who said, 'Out of darkness the light shall shine!' is the same God who made his light shine in our hearts, to bring us the knowledge of God's glory shining in the face of Christ."* (TEV)

2 Peter 1:3-4 – *"As we know Jesus better, his divine power gives us everything we need for living a godly life. He has called us to receive his own glory and goodness! And by that same mighty power, he has given us all of his rich and wonderful promises. He has promised that you will escape the decadence all around you caused by evil desires and that you will share in his divine nature."*

Partaking of God's glorious nature only happens in our union with Christ. For "in Him are hid all the treasures of wisdom and knowledge," and "in Him dwells the fullness of the Godhead bodily."

Eph. 1:3 – *"Let us give thanks to the God and Father of our Lord Jesus Christ! For in our union with Christ he has blessed us by giving us every spiritual blessing in the heavenly world."* (TEV)

Every blessing, including our salvation, that God has purposed for mankind is extended to us through one vehicle of grace alone. That vehicle of grace is none other than Jesus, the Eternal Word of the Living God, the second person of the Trinity.

That's why there is no salvation in any other religious belief system, be that Islam, Buddhism, Hinduism, the Occult, or any other religious practice.

Acts 4:12 – *"Salvation is found in no one else, for there is no other name under heaven given to men by which we must be saved."* (NIV)

I. The Revelation of God

1 Sam. 3:21-4:1 – *"Then the Lord **appeared again** in Shiloh. For **the Lord revealed Himself** to Samuel in Shiloh **by the word** of the Lord. And the word of Samuel came to **all Israel**."*

There are three levels of revelation that God has used to unveil Himself to mankind: **First**, is **General revelation** through the creation of all things; **second**, is **Special revelation** through the total text of Scripture; and the **third** means of revelation is in and through the person of His Son, Jesus, the Messiah.

God reveals Himself by making known or proclaiming His name. Scripture gives us a very clear revelation of the nature, character and attributes of God. Down through human history God has revealed His character and nature through His names.

To **worship** God is to call upon His name. To **reverence** God is to hallow His Holy name; and the Scripture also indicates that it is wickedness to take His name in vain.

There is a difference between the names of God and the attributes of God. The names of God express His whole being, while His attributes indicate the various sides of His character.

The Westminster Catechism summarizes the revelation of God in Scripture this way: "God is a Spirit, infinite, eternal, and unchangeable in His being, wisdom, power, holiness, justice, goodness and truth."

We know that God is Spirit! Therefore, when He chooses to reveal His person, He does so, Spirit to spirit. **[Refer to chapter 2 drawings of spirit, soul, & body on pages 18-19 – use the bull's-eye drawing]**

Notice, that there is a progression in the way God chooses to reveal Himself to His people, "Then the Lord **appeared again** in Shiloh."

On the first occasion, only **the Word of the Lord** was revealed to Samuel. The first time God spoke, Samuel made the mistake of thinking God's voice was the voice of Eli; however, by the fourth time God called, Samuel had gained a clear knowledge that the voice he was hearing was God's.

On this second occasion, the Holy Spirit uses the Word to reveal the very **character** and **nature** of God to Samuel.

Initially, I began to know the voice of the Lord in my spirit, which enabled me to begin functioning in the gifts of the Holy Spirit, such as prophecy; later, the Lord led me to open Paul's letter to the Philippians and He began to reveal His nature and character to me using this passage of Scripture.

Phil. 2:5-8 – *"Have this attitude in yourselves which was also in Christ Jesus, who, although He existed in the form of God, did not regard equality with God a thing to be grasped, but emptied Himself, taking the form of a bond-servant, and being made in the likeness of men. And being found in appearance as a man, He humbled Himself by becoming obedient to the point of death, even death on a cross."* (NASB)

Having read Paul's letter to the Philippians many times, I was familiar with that portion of Scripture. Plus, I had believed and given mental ascent to the truth that Jesus, the Eternal Word of God, came from heaven and in his human body had embraced the role of a servant and in humility embraced death on a cross for the sins of mankind.

But it wasn't until the Lord quickened that scripture to my heart causing it to explode in my spirit with revelation knowledge that I understood that this was His nature before He ever created the earth and everything in it. As long as Scripture is merely head knowledge, it cannot transform your life.

We must see the cross principle as revealed by the Holy Spirit and demonstrated by Jesus, as an **eternal** governing principle for our lives also.

Luke 9:23 – *"Then he said to them all: 'If anyone would come after me, he must deny himself and take up his cross daily and follow me.'"* (NIV)

Luke 14:26-27 – *"If anyone comes to me and does not hate his father and mother, his wife and children, his brothers and sisters--yes, even his own life--he cannot be my disciple. And anyone who does not carry his cross and follow me cannot be my disciple."* (NIV)

The "cross" was not just something Jesus was willing to suffer in order to redeem us from our sins; the cross is a principle in the eternal character and nature of God. Speaking of his soon death on the cross, Jesus said, *"I am telling you the truth: a grain of wheat remains no more than a single grain unless it is dropped into the ground and dies. If it does die, then it produces many grains."* John 12:24 (TEV)

Now, it is not insignificant that on both occasions when God reveals Himself to Samuel that it was in Shiloh. Shiloh means "rest." Do you know what it means to enter the rest of God?

Heb. 3:19-4:2, 9-11 – *"So we see that they were not able to enter, because of their unbelief. Therefore, since the promise of entering his rest still stands, let us be careful that none of you be found to have fallen short of it. For we also have had the gospel preached to us, just as they did; but the message they heard was of no value to them, because those who heard did not combine it with faith. There remains, then, a Sabbath-rest for the people of God; for **anyone who enters God's rest** also **rests from his own work**, just as God did from his. Let us, therefore, **make every effort** to enter that rest, so that no one will fall by following their example of disobedience."*

Entering God's rest is learning to cease from laboring in the energy of the flesh and allowing the Holy Spirit to energize you to do the will of God. Paul learned this wonderful truth and shared it with the Colossian believers. (NKJV)

Col. 1:28-29 – *"So everywhere we go, we tell everyone about Christ. We warn them and teach them with all the wisdom God has given us, for we want to present them to God, perfect in their relationship to Christ. I work very hard at this, as **I depend on Christ's mighty power** that works within me."*

II. God's Word Permeates All Israel

1 Sam. 4:1 – *"And the word of Samuel came to **all Israel**."*

Rom. 1:16-17 – *"For I am not ashamed of the gospel of Christ: for it is the power of God unto salvation to everyone that believeth; to the Jew first, and also to the Greek. For therein is the righteousness of God revealed **from faith to faith**: as it is written, 'The just shall live by faith.'"* (NKJV)

We all know that growth in Christ or growing in the knowledge of God is a progressive experience "from faith to faith". So, when the Scripture describes the fact that all Israel received the Word of Samuel, we can envision God's Word progressively touching and confronting every area of our lives, especially those areas where we may be experiencing bondage or areas in which God knows we need to be set free from sin's influence and control.

As we read, study, and meditate upon God's Word, the Holy Spirit uses it to confront attitudes, thought patterns, and behaviors that are contrary to the nature of God and that hinder the release of Christ's life within us.

On our own, we are unable to discern the true condition of our heart.

Jer. 17:9-10 – *"The heart is the most deceitful thing there is and desperately wicked. No one can really know how bad it is! Only the Lord knows! He searches all hearts and examines deepest motives so he can give to each person his right reward, according to his deeds--how he has lived."* (LB)

The Apostle James tells us that as we look into the Word it acts like a mirror to help us see what is on the inside of our heart. (James 1:22-25)

Heb. 4:12 – *"The word of God is something alive and active: it cuts more incisively than any two-edged sword: it can seek out the place where soul is divided from spirit, or joints from marrow; it can pass judgment on secret emotions and thoughts."* (NJB)

God uses His Word to renew our minds and transform the way we think and live, so we can demonstrate His good and acceptable and perfect will for our lives. (Rom. 12:2)

When we initially come to Christ repenting of our sinful independence and receive Him as Lord and Savior, God takes for granted that we are committed to eating the whole loaf, which is Christ. He is the Bread of Life.

As we begin to learn of Christ (for all truth is in Jesus), God doesn't cram the entire loaf of Christ, the bread of life, down our throats; rather, we partake of Christ bite by bite, little by little. (Eph. 4:21)

As Jesus said to his disciples, *"Oh, there is so much more I want to tell you, but you can't bear it now."* (John 16:12)

We also need to notice that Samuel becomes the source of God's living Word to Israel, the believer. In other words, God's Word comes to us through the Spirit of Christ dwelling in our human spirit.

If we don't allow the Holy Spirit to quicken God's Word to our hearts, we will simply be spending our time focusing on dead letter, instead of receiving from the life-giving Spirit.

Unbelievers as well as believers read the Bible; and to the unregenerate, it is merely dead letter or some well-written history of the Jews. To the believer, who has the Holy Spirit dwelling within, the Word can be quickened to his or her heart allowing for life-altering transformation to take place.

III. Spiritual Warfare – The Inevitable Battle

1 Sam. 4:1 – *"Now Israel went out against the **Philistines**, and encamped beside Ebenezer; and the Philistines encamped in Aphek."*

As I stated in chapter 3, the Philistines represent the external enemy (Satan and demonic powers). When they come against us as believers, we must rise up against them and do battle. We cannot afford to run because our protective armor, as described in Ephesians chapter six, merely covers our front side, not our backside.

Spiritual warfare is inevitable for every believer. Satan is working through the deception of the world-system to lead us away from God into self-willed independence.

Once we're separated from God, we're vulnerable to Satan's attack. He will tempt us by urging us to fulfill the lusts of our flesh, he will try to deceive us into believing that personal glory and people's approval is more important than God's approval, and he will try to deceive us into thinking that the accumulation of worldly goods is what gives us value as a person.

So, when it comes to understanding our warfare, God uses the **physical** battles fought by Israel to teach us about the **spiritual** battles we will definitely face as New Testament believers.

The Apostle Paul described it this way:

1 Cor. 10:11 – *"All these events happened to them as examples for us. They were written down to warn us, who live at the time when this age is drawing to a close."*

Eph. 6:12 – *"For our struggle is not against flesh and blood, but against the rulers, against the authorities, against the powers of this dark world and against the spiritual forces of evil in the heavenly realms."* (NIV)

Paul in describing the many spiritual battles he faced while serving Christ, in his letter to the Corinthian believers, says:

2 Cor. 11:23-28 – *"I have worked much harder, been in prison more frequently, been flogged more severely, and been exposed to death again and again. Five times I received from the Jews the forty lashes minus* one. *Three times I was beaten with rods, once I was stoned, three times I was shipwrecked, I spent a night and a day in the open sea, I have been constantly on the move. I have been in danger from rivers, in danger from bandits, in danger from my own countrymen, in danger from Gentiles; in danger in the city, in danger in the country, in danger at sea; and in danger from false brothers. I have labored and toiled and have often gone without sleep; I have known hunger and thirst and have often gone without food; I have been cold and naked. Besides everything else, I face daily the pressure of my concern for all the churches."* (NIV)

This constant buffeting and persecution of Paul was Satan's attempt to discourage Paul and keep him from fulfilling God's will for his life. But what did it teach Paul?

2 Cor. 1:8-10 – *"I think you ought to know, dear brothers and sisters, about the trouble we went through in the province of Asia. We were crushed and completely overwhelmed, and we thought we would never live through it. In fact, we expected to die. But **as a result**, **we learned not to rely on ourselves**, but on God who can raise the dead. And he did deliver us from mortal danger. And we are confident that he will continue to deliver us."*

Learning **not** to trust in your self is a very important lesson; however, what do we trust in?

IV. Misplaced Trust Ends in The Defeat of The Believer

1 Sam. 4:2-3 – *"And when they joined battle, **Israel was defeated** by the Philistines, who killed about four thousand men of the army in the field. And when the people had come into the camp, the elders of Israel said, 'Why has the Lord defeated us today before the Philistines? Let us bring **the ark of the covenant** of the Lord from Shiloh to us, that when it comes among us **it may save us** from the hand of our enemies.'"* (NKJV)

Do you ever think Paul questioned why God allowed the experiences of defeat into his life? Of course he did!

2 Cor. 12:6-9 – *"I don't want anyone to think more highly of me than what they can actually see in my life and my message, even though I have received* *wonderful revelations from God. But to keep me from getting puffed up, I was given a thorn in my flesh, a messenger from Satan to torment me and keep me from getting proud.*

Three different times I begged the Lord to take it away. Each time he said, 'My gracious favor is all you need. My power works best in your weakness.' So now I am glad to boast about my weaknesses, so that the power of Christ may work through me."

Defeated by the Philistines, Israel immediately looked for an answer and concluded that the answer was in the Ark of the Covenant, which is a type of God's Law Word.

Have you ever been stumped by a problem or a difficulty in your life and gone to the Word for the answer or solution?

You could be facing broken relationships, disobedient children, or a financial shortfall, and as Christians we often go to God's Word for help and end up confessing: "I'm standing on God's Word."

There is, however, a problem for many who make a confession of standing on God's Word. Jesus pointed this problem out when he told the parable of the Sower. In that parable Jesus tells us that 75% of the Word which people hear does them no good.

Matt. 13:19-21 – *"When anyone hears the message about the kingdom and does not understand it, the evil one comes and snatches away what was sown in his heart. This is the seed sown along the path. The one who received the seed that fell on rocky places is the man who hears the word and at once receives it with joy. But since he has no root, he lasts only a short time. When trouble or persecution comes because of the word, he quickly falls away."* (NIV)

So, why doesn't the message bring profit to the listener? The answer is seen in verse 4:

1 Sam. 4:4 – *"So the people sent to Shiloh, that they might bring from there the ark of the covenant of the Lord of hosts, who dwells between the cherubim. And the two sons of Eli, **Hophni and Phinehas, were there with the ark** of the covenant of God."* (NKJV)

When our flesh is handling the Word of God and we're standing on God's promises in the energy of the flesh, the Word is simply "dead letter" to us. And we can quote the scripture until we're blue in the face and it will avail us nothing. Notice verse 5:

1 Sam. 4:5 – *"And when the ark of the covenant of the Lord came into the camp, **all Israel shouted** so loudly, that the **earth shook**."* (NKJV)

All the emotional hype in the world, whether it's pumped up by the worship leader or by the choir director amounts to nothing. You can raise the roof, but as long as Hophni and Phinehas are the ones carrying the Ark, it is all for naught.

Here's the secret to victory and success in the midst of battle: The Word must bring us to Jesus and our trust must be in Him.

When presented with the concept that salvation, deliverance, and eternal life come from understanding the Scriptures, Jesus simply replied, *"You search the Scriptures because you believe they give you eternal life. But the Scriptures point to me! Yet you refuse to come to me so that I can give you this eternal life."* John 5:39-40 (NLT)

Brothers and sisters, Jesus is the Captain of our salvation. We do not save ourselves by trusting in some Bible verse as though it were some fetish worn around our neck.

Acts 4:12 – *"Jesus is the only One who can save people. His name is the only power in the world that has been given to save people. We must be saved through him."* (NCV)

V. God's Method of Deliverance – Suffering and Defeat

1 Sam. 4:6, 10-11 – *"Now when the Philistines heard the noise of the shout, they said, 'What does the sound of this great shout in the camp of the Hebrews mean?' Then they understood that the ark of the Lord had come into the camp.*

So the Philistines fought, and Israel was defeated, and every man fled to his tent. There was a very great slaughter, and there fell of Israel thirty thousand foot soldiers. Also the ark of God was captured; and the two sons of Eli, Hophni and Phinehas, died." (NKJV)

While Samuel was being established in Israel as the source for the Word of the Lord to the nation, the Philistines attacked Israel about 25 miles west of Shiloh at Aphek. In the initial encounter, Israel loses about 4,000 men and it became clear that the Philistines were winning the battle, so the Israelites sent for the Ark of the Covenant to be brought to the battlefield.

They superstitiously supposed that its presence, like some good-luck charm, would turn the tide. Even the Philistines were terrified when they knew the Ark was in the camp of Israel, for they had heard about Israel's victories in Egypt more than 300 years before.

The **Philistines were fearful** based on the reputation of God's deliverance through Moses. On the other hand, **the Israelites were overly confident** based on the past reputation of God's deliverance.

So what that means is, if we think we can just open the Bible, a book that contains the promises of the Lord and find one that seems to fit our situation, that isn't going to be enough.

The promises of God's written Word must bring us to hearing Christ's voice in our spirit, producing a living faith in Jesus.

Trusting in the presence of the Ark (the dead letter of Scripture) Israel went forth into battle and once again was defeated by their enemies, with every man fleeing to his tent.

In the process of Israel's defeat, the Ark was captured and the sons of Eli, its keepers, were slain. Now, when Eli learned that the Philistine army had captured the Ark and that his sons had been slain, he fell backward off his seat, broke his neck, and died.

Shortly thereafter, Phinehas' wife died following the birth of a son whom she named Ichabod, meaning, "The glory is departed."

Since the Ark represented both God's abiding presence and the written Word of God in Israel, its capture would appear to signify that worldly philosophies had become most powerful, making God Himself and all His glory irrelevant.

Ever heard of the "God is dead" theology? If I remember correctly, it was one of the Beatles who declared their rising popularity was a confirmation of the death of Christianity.

Skeptics have proclaimed a simple argument within college halls for centuries:

1. If God is all-good. He *would,* destroy evil.
2. If God is all-powerful. He *could* destroy evil.
3. But evil is not destroyed.
4. Hence, there is no such God.

So, why hasn't God done something about our sin nature, which produces all the evil in the world? In fact, evil appears to be persistently growing.

The **first** thing we need to understand is inherent evil cannot be destroyed without destroying man's freedom. By one man, Adam, a freewill being, sin has entered the world. Freewill beings are the cause of evil, and freedom was given to us so that we could express true love. Jesus was asked:

Matt. 22:36-39 – *"Teacher, what is the most important commandment in the Law? Jesus answered: 'Love the Lord your God with all your heart, soul, and mind. This is the first and most important commandment. The second most important commandment is like this one. And it is, Love others as much as you love yourself.'"* (CEV)

Love is the greatest good for all free creatures, but love is impossible without freedom. So, if freedom were destroyed, ending the possibility of performing evil acts; that would be evil in itself, because it would deprive creatures of their greatest good – the free choice to love.

Hence, to destroy evil would actually be evil. If evil is to be overcome, we need to talk about it being defeated, not destroyed.

This argument against God arrogantly assumes that just because evil is not destroyed right now, it never will be. The argument implies that if God hasn't done anything as of today, then it won't ever happen. But this assumes that the person making the argument has some inside information about the future.

However, if we restate the argument to correct this oversight in temporal perspective, it turns out to be an argument that actually vindicates God.

1 If God is all-good. He will defeat evil.
2 If God is all-powerful. He can defeat evil.
3. Evil is not *yet* defeated.
4. Therefore, God *can* and *will one day* utterly defeat evil.

The very argument used against the existence of God turns out to be a vindication of God in the face of the problem of evil. God isn't finished yet. The final chapter has not been fulfilled.

God is love, so when He created the heavens and the earth, He created it "good." God is also "Light and Truth."

1 John 1:5-6 – *"This is the message he has given us to announce to you: God is light and there is no darkness in him at all. So we are lying if we say we have fellowship with God but go on living in spiritual darkness. We are not living in the truth."*

In the beginning God separated the light from the darkness, an act, which directly corresponds to His nature. There is NO darkness in God.

1 Tim. 6:15-16 – *"For in due season Christ will be revealed from heaven by the blessed and only Almighty God, the King of kings and Lord of lords, who alone can never die, who lives in light so terrible that no human being can approach him. No mere man has ever seen him nor ever will. Unto him be honor and everlasting power and dominion forever and ever. Amen."* (LB)

When Adam sinned in the garden, he made a freewill choice to embrace the knowledge of good and evil. In so doing, he forsook the opportunity to eat of the tree of Life (God's nature).

However, through redemption in Christ, we now have the opportunity to repent of our sinful behavior and die to sin (the rebellious nature) through our identification with Jesus Christ in his death, burial, and resurrection and become partakers of God's divine nature. (Rom. 6)(1 Pet. 1:2-4)

We know that God has already dealt with evil in two ways: **first**, by placing on Christ the sins of the whole world. Through Christ's suffering and death, he paid the penalty for our sins. **Second**, Christ dealt with our sin nature, which has been the source of our sinful behavior.

Through the regeneration of our spirit we have been given a new nature from Christ and through our identification with Him in His death, burial, and resurrection, we have been freed from the domination of the old sinful nature in order that we may walk in newness of life by God's glory.

Jesus said: *"I am the light of the world. Whoever follows me will never walk in darkness, but will have the light of life."* **John 8:12** (NIV)

John 12:46 – *"I have come into the world as a light, so that no one who believes in me should stay in darkness."* (NIV)

Understanding that God has separated darkness far from Himself and not only dwells in light, but is the Light, and that Jesus Christ is Light, what is God's will for His redeemed people?

1 Pet. 2:9 – *"But you are a chosen people, a royal priesthood, a holy nation, a people belonging to God, that you may declare the praises of him who called you out of darkness into his wonderful light."* (NIV)

Eph. 5:8-9 – *"For though your hearts were once full of darkness, now you are full of light from the Lord, and your behavior should show it! For this light within you produces only what is good and right and true."* (NLT)

So, we are not only to dwell in the light of God's living Word, but we are also to be filled with God's Word expressing the light of God's nature. Peter declares God's wonderful purpose for us in his second epistle:

2 Peter 1:2-4 – *"May God bless you with his special favor and wonderful peace as you come to know Jesus, our God and Lord, better and better. As we know Jesus better, his divine power gives us everything we need for living a godly life. He has called us to receive his own glory and goodness! And by that same mighty power, he has given us all of his rich and wonderful promises. He* *has promised that you will escape the decadence all around you caused by evil desires and that you will share in his divine nature."* (NLT)

So, if it is God's will for us as freewill beings to choose to walk in the light and be children of light, loving God and one another, how does God actually work in our lives to bring this about?

2 Cor. 1:8-10 – *"I think you ought to know, dear brothers and sisters, about the trouble we went through in the province of Asia.* **We were crushed and completely overwhelmed**, *and we thought we would never live through it. In fact, we expected to die. But* **as a result**, **we learned not to rely on ourselves**, *but on God who can raise the dead. And he did deliver us from mortal danger. And we are confident that he will continue to deliver us."* (NLT)

Paul's experience, then, was no different from ours today. He learned to depend upon the Lord by virtue of the troubles he faced in life. Crushed, overwhelmed, and expecting to die, he was delivered from trusting in self and learned to rely on God, who can raise the dead.

Anyone who suffers asks, "WHY" "Why did I lose my leg?" "Why did our church burn down?" "Why did my little girl have to die?" "WHY?" Unfortunately, we can't always give an answer that satisfies the souls of those who hurt or even help them make sense of their pain.

But for anyone who uses the world's rationale to deny God's existence or goodness, we can give them an answer.

They rationalize:

1. There is no good purpose for suffering.
2. A truly good God must have a good purpose for everything.
3. So, there cannot be a truly good God.

However, there is a difference between our **knowing the purpose** for suffering, defeat, and loss, and God **having a purpose** for it. Even when we don't know God's purpose, He may still have a good reason for allowing defeat and suffering to touch our lives. So we can't assume that there is no good purpose for something just because we don't know what it could be.

We do know some of God's purposes for suffering. For instance, we know that God sometimes uses pain to warn us of greater evils. Anyone who has raised a child has gone through the months of fearing that the baby might touch a hot stove or drink a scalding cup of tea for the first time.

We hate to think of it, but we know that once the child touches something hot, he will instantly have an existential awareness of the meaning of the word "hot" and will immediately respond when we use it.

That first small pain is allowed to avoid the danger of bigger ones later on.

Pain can also keep us from self-destruction. Do you know why lepers lose their fingers, toes, and noses? Usually, it has nothing directly to do with the leprosy itself. Rather, the disease causes them to lose feeling in their extremities, and they literally injure themselves. They can't feel the pain when they touch a hot pan, so they hang on to it until it burns them.

Without feeling things that they are about to bump into, they hit them full force without slowing down. Without the sensation of pain, they do tremendous damage to themselves and don't even realize it.

> Dr. Paul Brand, a leading researcher and therapist of Hansen's disease, expressed significant insights on the problem of pain. Having just examined three patients, **Lou**—who may lose his thumb to infection from playing the autoharp. **Hector**—who can't feel the damage he is doing to his hand while mopping, and **Jose**—who is unwilling to wear special shoes to prevent the loss of the nubs that were once his feet.

> Dr. Brand says this:

> Pain—it's often seen as the great inhibitor, which ropes off certain activities. But I see it as the great giver of freedom. Look at these men. **Lou**: we're desperately searching for a way to give him simple freedom to play an autoharp. **Hector**: he can't even mop a floor without harming himself. **Jose**: too proud for proper treatment, he's given a makeshift shoe, which may keep him from losing even more of his feet. He can't dress nicely and walk normally: for that, he would need the gift of pain. [From *Where Is God When It Hurts?* by Philip Yancey [(Grand Rapids: Zondervan, 1977), p. 37]

While it may seem like a high price to pay, some suffering helps to bring about greater good. The Bible gives several examples of this in men like Joseph, Job, and Samson. Each went through real suffering.

How would the nation of Israel have survived the famine if Joseph had not been sold into slavery by his brothers and imprisoned unjustly?

Would Job have been able to make his marked spiritual growth had he not suffered first? (Job 23:10)

What kind of leader would the Apostle Paul have been if he had not been humbled after his exalted revelations from God? (2 Cor. 12)

Joseph summarized the matter when he told his brothers, "As far as I am concerned, God turned into good what you meant for evil. He brought me to the high position I have today so I could save the lives of many people." (Gen. 50:20)

Projects like the "Scared Straight" program at Rahway Prison have stopped many young people from following a life of crime, but the convicts who tell them about prison life have both caused suffering and experienced suffering.

And then there is the ultimate example: **the Cross**. Apparently, an infinite injustice was wrought on an innocent Man so that good might come to all.

The evil that He endured as our substitute allows us free access to God without fear, because our guilt and punishment have been taken away.

Why would God allow His own Son to suffer a cruel and violent death as a criminal when He had done nothing wrong? You see, this injustice is very hard to explain unless there is some greater good accomplished by Christ's death, which overshadows the evil of it.

Jesus' own explanation was that He had come *"to give His life [as] a ransom for many"* (Mark 10:45) and saying, *"Greater love has no one than this, that one lay down his life for his friends"* (John 15:13).

Hebrews 12:2 states the purpose of Jesus, *"who for the joy set before Him endured the cross, despising the shame,"* meaning that the reconciliation of sinners was worth the suffering.

As Isaiah says, *"He was pierced through for our transgressions. He was crushed for our iniquities; the chastening for our well-being fell upon Him, and by His scourging we are healed"* (Isa. 53:5).

The higher purpose and greater good derived from Christ's death as our substitute for the penalty of our sins is more important than the evil inherent in the process.

C.S. Lewis said, "God **whispers** to us in our pleasures, **speaks** in our conscience, but **shouts** in our pains: it is His megaphone to rouse a deaf world."

In some sense, we need pain, so we are not overcome by the evil that we would choose, were it painless. In the face of the enemies attack, the strength of the flesh, represented in Hophni and Phinehas, fails. The flesh's manipulating and scheming powers availed for nothing. Fleshly wisdom and religious philosophy availed for nothing.

It was their utter disregard for God and His revealed Word that proved to be their downfall.

What does God say?

Isaiah 55:7-9 – *"**Let the wicked forsake his way** and **the evil man his thoughts**. Let him turn to the Lord, and he will have mercy on him, and to our God, for he will freely pardon. 'For my thoughts are not your thoughts, neither are your ways my ways,' declares the Lord. 'As the heavens are higher than the earth, so are my ways higher than your ways and my thoughts than your thoughts."* (NIV)

When the Scripture refers to a person as wicked or evil, that does not mean that person has committed every crime in the book. It is simply stating, *"There is no one righteous, not even one"* Rom. 3:10. *"We have all sinned and fallen short of God's glorious standard"* Rom. 3:23.

What we fail to realize is that we were born with a sin nature and the vast majority of knowledge we retain has come from our five senses, therefore, we are already conformed to this world-system in more ways than we comprehend.

The reality is that there is wickedness and evil in every heart and if unchecked by the renewing of our mind with the Word of God, that wickedness will eventually manifest itself.

Turning to the Lord for mercy and pardon and clearly identifying with our new life in Christ is the means by which we bring unclean thoughts into captivity and forsake our old ways.

When David brought the Ark of God up from the home of Abinadab, he placed it on a new cart and Uzzah and Ahio were guiding the Ark. When the Ark became unsteady and began to fall, Uzzah reached out to steady the Ark of God's presence and was slain.

Why was Uzzah slain? He was slain because he disregarded the instruction of God's Word to his ancestors about how to carry the Ark. Uzzah concluded that it was easier on his flesh if the ox carried the Ark instead of him. He thought his way was better than God's way.

Gal. 6:7-8 – *"Do not be deceived: God cannot be mocked. A man reaps what he sows. The one who sows to please his sinful nature, from that nature will reap destruction; the one who sows to please the Spirit, from the Spirit will reap eternal life."* (NIV)

Once Israel had entered servitude and began to suffer oppression under the hand of Pharaoh in Egypt, what was the anticipated response? That the people of Israel would cry out to God for deliverance. And that's exactly what they did.

Down through Israel's history, God has continually used the judgment of foreign attack and oppression to provoke a cry for help from His covenant people.

Regardless of why the attack came, whether from disobedience and the worship of false gods or simply from God's desire to show Himself mighty to save; in any case, God used suffering to teach His people to return to the Lord and put their trust in Him. In fact:

Heb. 5:8 – *"Even though Jesus was God's Son, he learned obedience from the things he suffered."*

In coming to grips with the truth of understanding God's ways, Paul said:

2 Cor. 4:7-12 – *"But this precious treasure—this light and power that now shine within us—is held in perishable containers, that is, in our weak bodies. So everyone can see that our glorious power is from God and is not our own. We are pressed on every side by troubles, but we are not crushed and broken. We are perplexed, but we don't give up and quit. We are hunted down, but God never abandons us. We get knocked down, but we get up again and keep going. Through suffering, these bodies of ours constantly share in the death of Jesus so that the life of Jesus may also be seen in our bodies. Yes, we live under constant danger of death because we serve Jesus, so that the life of Jesus will be obvious in our dying bodies. So we live in the face of death, but it has resulted in eternal life for you."* (NLT)

Once we grasp this truth that God's ways are not our ways, we become open to learning that God uses suffering and defeat to bring glorious deliverance into our lives. For this we praise His Holy name.

Prayer: Father, we thank you for teaching us to listen for your voice and to recognize the witness of the Holy Spirit confirming your word to our hearts. You have taught us that every one of us will face the conflict of spiritual warfare and so you have instructed us to put on the whole armor of God so that we might withstand the schemes of the devil.

Today, you are helping us understand that we can't just "name it and claim it" or grab a scripture and "stand on it," expecting immediate miracles. Rather, you have given us your Word to bring us to Jesus. May we learn to trust in Jesus for your glory, we pray. Amen!

CHAPTER TEN

The Authority of God's Word over the Sin Nature

<u>1 Sam. 4:10-18</u> – *"So the Philistines fought, and Israel **was defeated**, and every man fled to his tent. There was a very great slaughter, and there fell of Israel thirty thousand foot soldiers. Also, the **ark of God was captured**; and the two sons of Eli, **Hophni and Phinehas, died**.*

*Then a man of Benjamin ran from the battle line the same day, and came to Shiloh with his **clothes torn and dirt on his head**. Now when he came, there was Eli, **sitting on a seat** by the **wayside watching**, for his heart **trembled for the ark** of God. And when the man came into the city and told it, all the city cried out. When Eli heard the noise of the outcry, he said, "What does the sound of this tumult mean?" And the man came quickly and told Eli. Eli was ninety-eight years old, and his eyes were so dim that **he could not see**.*

Then the man said to Eli, "I am he who came from the battle. And I fled today from the battle line."

And he said, "What happened, my son?"

*So the messenger answered and said, "Israel **has fled** before the Philistines, and there has been a great slaughter among the people. Also your two sons, **Hophni and Phinehas, are dead**; and **the ark of God has been captured**."*

*Then it happened, when he made mention of the ark of God, that **Eli fell off the seat** backward by the side of the gate; and his neck was broken and*

he died, *for the man was old and heavy. And he had **judged Israel forty years**.*" (NKJV)

I. God's Path to Freedom

Living free from the domination of our flesh is God's plan for every believer in Christ.

Gal. 5:1 – *"It is for freedom that Christ has set us free. Stand firm, then, and do not let yourselves be burdened again by a yoke of slavery."* (NIV)

Gal. 5:13 – *"It is absolutely clear that God has called you to a free life. Just make sure that you don't use this freedom as an excuse to do whatever you want to do and destroy your freedom. Rather, use your freedom to serve one another in love; that's how freedom grows."* (Msg)

Previously we were reminded that the greatest commandment and man's highest good is to love God with all our heart, mind, soul, and strength; and also to love others as much as we love ourselves. We also learned it is impossible to demonstrate this kind of love, without freewill.

Since freewill allows for the sin nature to be expressed in the earth, our problem is how to deal with the evil our sin nature initiates. We can't destroy it, because to destroy the possibility of evil is to destroy the reality of freewill, which is necessary for loving God properly.

So, rather than eradicating the possibility of evil, God has, instead, given us the ability, in Christ, to defeat evil and to actually rule over our sinful flesh nature. (Rom. 6-8)

To live free from the domination of our fallen sin nature, we must walk in a freedom that only Jesus can produce in us. God is giving to all true believers the heart Jesus demonstrated *"he loved righteousness and hated wickedness."* (Heb. 1:9)

John 8:36 – *"So if the Son sets you free, you will be free indeed."* (NIV)

Freedom is the result of receiving and coming to know Jesus Christ as Savior, Lord and life, and submitting to the instruction of His Word.

John 8:32 – *"Then you will know the truth, and the truth will set you free."* (NIV)

So, how does God actually deliver us from the dominance of our fleshly sin nature, which produces sinful acts in our lives?

1 Sam. 4:10 – *"So the Philistines fought, and [again] **Israel was defeated**."*

Humility and brokenness has never been considered "the best path" in reaching the top of the corporate ladder of success. People just don't want the path to greatness to include suffering and defeat.

And yet, when you talk to the vast majority of people who have succeeded in finding God's purpose for their life, you find it was realized only after experiencing difficulties, hardship, or even a major crisis.

Jesus has defeated Satan, along with the consequences of sin and death through His own death on the cross and subsequent resurrection. And as people of faith, we enter into that victory through our identification with Christ.

By embracing our own personal cross and dying daily to self-will, we share in Christ's sufferings and we actually learn obedience through the things, which we suffer. The ending result is that we get to become "partakers of His divine nature." (2 Pet. 1:4).

II. Weeping for the Wrong Thing

1 Sam. 4:12 – *"Then a man of Benjamin ran from the battle line the same day, and came to Shiloh with his **clothes torn and dirt on his head**."*

The Scripture says, when God's judgments are manifest in the earth, "men will learn righteousness" (Isa. 26:9). The traditional Middle Eastern method of expressing the fact that you are in mourning was to tear your clothes and pour dirt or ashes on your head. So, the question arises: why is this man of Benjamin mourning?

When something goes wrong and life seems to take a turn for the worst, do you weep and mourn for the wrong thing? Note Samuel's response regarding Saul:

1 Sam. 15:34-16:1 – *"Then Samuel left for Ramah, but Saul went up to his home in Gibeah of Saul. Until the day Samuel died, he did not go to see Saul again, though Samuel mourned for him. And the Lord was grieved that he had made Saul king over Israel.*

The Lord said to Samuel, 'How long will you mourn for Saul, since I have rejected him as king over Israel? Fill your horn with oil and be on your way; I am sending you to Jesse of Bethlehem. I have chosen one of his sons to be king.'" (NIV)

Do we mourn because our hopes were dashed, or do we mourn because God's name is not being glorified?

When Israel cried out in their bondage in Egypt, their mourning was appropriate (Ex. 2:23). But when Israel cried out for meat to eat, their weeping was not appropriate. Why not?

Num. 11:1-6, 10 – *"The people soon began to complain to the Lord about their hardships; and when the Lord heard them, his anger blazed against them. Fire from the Lord raged among them and destroyed the outskirts of the camp. The people screamed to Moses for help; and when he prayed to the Lord, the fire stopped. After that, the area was known as Taberah—"the place of burning"—because fire from the Lord had burned among them there.*

Then the foreign rabble who were traveling with the Israelites began to crave the good things of Egypt, and the people of Israel also began to complain. 'Oh, for some meat!' they exclaimed. 'We remember all the fish we used to eat for free in Egypt. And we had all the cucumbers, melons, leeks, onions, and garlic that we wanted.

But now our appetites are gone, and day after day we have nothing to eat but this manna!' Moses heard all the families standing in front of their tents weeping, and the Lord became extremely angry. Moses was also very aggravated."

Num. 25:1-13 – *"While the Israelites were camped at Acacia, some of the men defiled themselves by sleeping with the local Moabite women. These women invited them to attend sacrifices to their gods, and soon the Israelites* *were feasting with them and worshiping the gods of Moab. Before long Israel was joining in the worship of Baal of Peor, causing the Lord's anger to blaze against his people.*

The Lord issued the following command to Moses: 'Seize all the ringleaders and execute them before the Lord in broad daylight, so his fierce anger will turn away from the people of Israel.' So Moses ordered Israel's judges to execute everyone who had joined in worshiping Baal of Peor.

Just then one of the Israelite men brought a Midianite woman into the camp, right before the eyes of Moses and all the people, as they were weeping at the entrance of the Tabernacle. When Phinehas son of Eleazar and grandson of Aaron the priest saw this, he jumped up and left the assembly. Then he took a spear and rushed after the man into his tent. Phinehas thrust the spear all the way through the man's body and into the woman's stomach. So the plague against the Israelites was stopped, but not before 24,000 people had died.

Then the Lord said to Moses, "Phinehas son of Eleazar and grandson of Aaron the priest has turned my anger away from the Israelites by displaying passionate zeal among them on my behalf. So I have stopped destroying all Israel as I had intended to do in my anger. So tell him that I am making my special covenant of peace with him. In this covenant, he and his descendants will be priests for all time, because he was zealous for his God and made atonement for the people of Israel."

Here's the million dollar question: When we are upset and we weep and mourn, is it because we're sad that we have to experience suffering and defeat, not knowing why it has to happen; or do we get upset, and weep and mourn, because we are jealous for God's honor and glory?

It was jealousy for God's honor and glory that Jesus cleansed the Temple and then wept over Jerusalem because of their unbelief. Are you and I weeping for the right reasons?

Too often, when we don't understand God's ways, we weep and mourn for the wrong reasons.

III. God's Word Is Taken Captive – Hope Dispelled

1 Sam. 4:17 – *"Also **the ark of God was captured**."*

Mark 7:13 – *"In this way the teaching you pass on to others cancels out the word of God. And there are many other things like this that you do."* (TEV)

Jesus rebuked the Pharisees for establishing teachings that actually allowed people an excuse for disobeying God's word.

Have you ever allowed secular reasoning or religious traditions (the way you, your ancestors, or society have done it for years) to capture and make ineffective God's Word for your life?

Today, untold numbers of Christian youth have left their Christian homes to enter a college or university and sit under the tutelage of godless professors. In so doing, they have too often ended up discarding their knowledge of God's Word for a secular education. They have allowed worldly philosophies to be exalted over God's eternal Word.

Exalting worldly rationalizations above the revealed truth of God's word makes God's word irrelevant for life application and impotent to bring about godly change in our lives.

Have you ever met someone who blamed God for the problems in their life?

I've heard people express their frustration with life's disappointments, "God didn't get me the job I wanted"; "God took my mother and then my little brother got sick, why did God let that happen."

Even people who initially trusted in Christ can become angry, bitter, and resentful and refuse to continue following the instruction of God's Word. And of course, that only ends up defiling their spirit and hindering their spiritual growth in God.

The apostle Paul talks to the Church about the importance of embracing the message of the cross.

1 Cor. 1:18-21 – *"I know very well how foolish the message of the cross sounds to those who are on the road to destruction. But we who are being saved* *recognize this message as the very power of God. As the Scriptures say, 'I will destroy human wisdom and discard their most brilliant ideas.' So where does this leave the philosophers, the scholars, and the world's brilliant debaters? God has made them all look foolish and has shown their wisdom to be useless nonsense. Since God in his wisdom saw to it that the world would never find him through human wisdom, he has used our foolish preaching to save all who believe."* (NLT)

When we refuse to accept suffering and defeat as part of God's plan to save, deliver, and set us free, we allow God's Word to be taken captive, forcing us to embrace erroneous conclusions.

Without the understanding of why suffering and defeat touch our lives, we lose our hope, our confidence, and the ability to trust God's Word and end up believing the enemy's lies.

We embrace an incorrect concept of God or a negative image of ourselves, we may then start believing that we're not worthy of God's mercy or we may conclude that God's Word isn't relevant for modern day cultures.

The message and principle of the cross is relevant for every generation. It is the very power of God to save us.

IV. God's Promise Is Fulfilled

<u>1 Sam. 4:17-18</u> – *"So the messenger answered and said, "**Israel has fled**... and there has been a great slaughter among the people. Also your two sons, **Hophni and Phinehas, are dead**... Then it happened, when he made mention of the ark of God, that **Eli fell off the seat** backward by the side of the gate; and his neck was broken and **he died**."*

God made a promise to Israel through Samuel that He was going to do something so marvelous in Israel that the ears of everyone who heard about it would 'tingle', or bear witness.

The sign that God gave to confirm He was going to raise up a faithful priest, who would do all that was in His heart and mind, was the death of Hophni and Phinehas in a single day.

God uses brokenness and defeat to enable us to quit trusting in self and that frees us from trusting human reason and the philosophies of the world, which produce the manifestation of the fruits of the flesh (Hophni and Phinehas).

In addition, we need to understand that God is truly committed to finish what He begins. And this God did, by removing Eli from his spiritual leadership position in Israel.

Praise God! He is a promise keeper. He watches over His Word to perform it!

V. The Time of Testing Has An End

1 Sam. 4:18 – *"And he had **judged Israel forty years**."*

At the mention of the capture of the Ark, Eli falls off his seat, breaks his neck and dies. He had judged (ruled and motivated) Israel for **40 years** (the time of testing and proving).

Too often, when we face tests and trials, like Job, we become God's critic and conclude that since we can't control the situation, it will probably just continue forever. Job saw no end in sight, yet all the time he was suffering, he longed to confront God face to face about his situation.

Then, when the opportunity finally presented itself, he was speechless.

Job 38:1-3 – *"Then the Lord answered Job from the whirlwind: 'Who is this that questions my wisdom with such ignorant words? Brace yourself, because I have some questions for you, and you must answer them."* (NLT)

Job 40:1-5 – *"Then the Lord said to Job, 'Do you still want to argue with the Almighty? You are God's critic, but do you have the answers?' Then Job replied to the Lord, 'I am nothing—how could I ever find the answers? I will put my hand over my mouth in silence. I have said too much already. I have nothing more to say."* (NLT)

In Genesis, God tested the inhabitants of the earth and He said:

Genesis 7:4 – *"One week from today I will begin **forty** days and **forty** nights of rain. And I will wipe from the earth all the living things I have created."* (NLT)

To the nation of Israel, He said:

Deut. 8:2, 16 – *"Remember how the Lord your God led you through the wilderness for **forty years**, humbling you and **testing you** to prove your character, and to find out whether or not you would really obey his commands. He fed you with manna in the wilderness, a food unknown to your ancestors. He did this to humble you and **test you** for your own good."* (NLT)

Judges 3:1 – *"The Lord left certain nations in the land **to test** those Israelites who had not participated in the wars of Canaan."* (NLT)

Psa. 66:10 – *"You have **tested** us, O God; you have purified us like silver melted in a crucible."* (NLT)

Psa. 105:19 – *"Until the time came to fulfill his word, the Lord **tested** Joseph's character."* (NLT)

Exodus 16:35 – *"The Israelites ate manna **forty** years, until they came to a land that was settled; they ate manna until they reached the border of Canaan."* (NIV)

At Kadesh-barnea, Israel was being ruled by the flesh, which seeks to save itself and the majority of the Israelites chose not to believe God's Word and so their testing continued.

Num. 14:33-34 – *"Your children will be shepherds here for forty years, suffering for your unfaithfulness, until the last of your bodies lies in the desert. For **forty years** – one year for each of the forty days you explored the land – you will suffer for your sins and know what it is like to have me against you."* (NIV)

Num. 32:13 – *"The Lord's anger burned against Israel and he made them wander in the desert **forty years**, until the whole generation of those who had done evil in his sight was gone."* (NIV)

The additional fact that Moses was exiled to the backside of the desert for 40 years, until God could free him from trusting in himself, helps us understand that the number 40 speaks to us as a type of testing from which we can learn a great deal.

For instance: Goliath was used of God to test Israel's courage. That testing would eventually call forth and reveal the man He had anointed to be the next king in Israel.

1 Sam. 17:16 – *"For **forty** days the Philistine came forward every morning and evening and took his stand."* (NIV)

When God sent the prophet Jonah to the wicked city of Nineveh, the city was designated a period of testing – 40 days. During that time of testing, God's Word produced a response of repentance, which God honored by staying His judgment for 100 years. (Jonah 3:4)

Being born again does not deliver us from the domination of our fallen, Adamic, sin nature. Instead, we have to go through the dealings of God and learn how to draw upon the life of Christ for the strength to live godly lives and rule over our rebellious flesh.

The process God takes us through includes suffering and defeat. During the process, we are tested so we can see what is truly in our hearts. The Word of God that dwells in our hearts will be challenged and for a time we may even become disheartened and lose hope.

But the testing time will come to an end, for God is faithful, even when we are not. And just as with Job, God will bring us forth victorious. He will heal us and give us a greater revelation of Himself than we could have otherwise ever known.

In the next chapter we will see that God uses His eternal Word to reveal Himself to mankind and to judge the hearts of men.

CHAPTER ELEVEN

The Judgment of God's Word

John 1:1-3 – *"In the beginning the Word already existed. He was with God, and he was God. He was in the beginning with God. He created everything there is. Nothing exists that he didn't make."* (NLT)

Heb. 4:12 – *"God's word is living and active. It is sharper than any two-edged sword and cuts as deep as the place where soul and spirit meet, the place where joints and marrow meet. God's word judges a person's thoughts and intentions."* (GW)

John 1:14 – *"So the Word became human and lived here on earth among us. He was full of unfailing love and faithfulness. And we have seen his glory, the glory of the only Son of the Father."* (NLT)

The revelation of God can be defined as the communication or exposure of His person, His will, and His redemptive activity. God has unveiled Himself to mankind on three different levels.

I. God's Presence in Creation.

The fact that it is "general" means that it is intended for all men of every age and every culture. Psalm 19 tells us "there is no speech nor language" where this revelation is not available.

General revelation declares the reality of the Creator-God. The reality of the Creator-God is clearly stated in Psalm 19 when it says, "the heavens declare the glory of God; and the firmament shows his handiwork."

The apostle Paul uses general revelation, in addressing the Greeks on Mars Hill, as a foundation and preparation for communicating God's "special" revelation.

Rom. 1:20 – *"For since the creation of the world God's invisible qualities – his eternal power and divine nature – have been clearly seen, being understood from what has been made, so that men are without excuse."* (NIV)

Man is not simply another part of the creation. He is unique in that man alone is made in the image of God. Man can never escape the theistic implications of his nature because he holds the truth of his origin within himself; however, his sin nature continually attempts to suppress this reality so that he can be his own "god," responsible only to himself.

The result of general revelation is that man has the witness of God's reality and existence both without and within, thus, man cannot escape the knowledge of God's existence. Man's attempted cover-up is to deny present day scientific evidence, which confirms God's intelligent design.[7]

Now because of Adam's sin, man is fallen and separated from his Creator and the reconciliation of man to God cannot be accomplished through general revelation, thus special revelation is needed.

II. The Special Revelation of God.

Because sin has limited our ability to understand God's self-revelation through creation, God has given us the special revelation of Himself through the writings of the apostles and prophets.

The Bible – a compilation of 40 different authors, written over 1500 years, carrying a singular, unified message – declares the majesty of God and the truth about His character. It declares His miraculous works in the earth and reveals His mysterious ways.

The Bible accomplishes several purposes: it reveals God through His activity in the affairs of men and it exposes the fallen character of humanity. It reveals our fallen predicament as being

---

7   Resource: THE PRIVILEGED PLANET, produced by Illustra Media, www. illustramedia.com

estranged from God through sinful rebellion and it reveals His saving solution in Christ.

From Abraham on, the nation of Israel was the recipient of God's special revelation that distinguished Israel from every other nation.

Rom. 3:2 – *"Yes, being a Jew has many advantages. First of all, the Jews were entrusted with the whole revelation of God."*

Deut. 4:5-6, 8 – *"I have taught you all the laws, as the Lord my God told me to do. Obey them in the land that you are about to invade and occupy. Obey them faithfully, and this will show the people of other nations how wise you are. When they hear of all these laws, they will say, 'What wisdom and understanding this great nation has!' No other nation, no matter how great, has laws so just as those that I have taught you today."* (TEV)

The Old Testament is the record of God's progressive revelatory and redemptive activity, culminating in the incarnation of Jesus, the Messiah.

In order for us to understand God's activity in the earth, we need the events of history to be accompanied by an interpretative word. Event and word must be nearly one, or the event itself will be misinterpreted or even worse, be meaningless to us.

Scripture, then, is the inspired word that accompanies the event giving us an inerrant interpretation of God's redemptive activity.

When the Word of God comes prior to the event, it is called prophecy and the fulfillment of prophecy was the express test of distinguishing between true and false prophets in Israel.

III. The Personification of General and Special Revelation

Heb. 1:1-3 – *"In the past God spoke to our forefathers through the prophets at many times and in various ways, but in these last days he has spoken to us by his Son, whom he appointed heir of all things, and through whom he made the universe. The Son is the radiance of God's glory and the exact representation of his being, sustaining all things by his powerful word. After* *he had provided purification for sins, he sat down at the right hand of the Majesty in heaven."* (NIV)

So, Christ is the final and supreme expression of revelation, the definitive Word of God. Thus, Scripture is the history, interpretation, and inerrant record of God's progressive revelation to man that culminates in God's own presence among men.

When Jesus ascended on high, he promised the disciples to send "the Spirit of truth" and ever since the day of Pentecost, all believers have been indwelt and anointed by the Holy Spirit so they could understand Scripture.

You cannot comprehend the authority of Christ and understand the power of His Word without accepting the authority of Scripture. What do I mean?

To fully comprehend the happenings described in 1 Samuel chapters 5 and 6, you must have an understanding of the power of God's Word resident, not only in the Bible, but even more so in Christ, the eternal Word of God.

Although there are numerous writings collected down through history, only certain writings are contained in the Bible. We call these writings "the canon of Scripture."

The word canon is of Christian origin, which means, "measuring rod" and later came to mean "a rule of faith."

"It should be understood, however, that the canonization of a book does not mean that the Jewish nation, in the one case, or the Christian Church, in the other, gave to that book its authority; but rather that its authority, being already established on other and sufficient grounds, it was in consequence recognized as properly belonging to the Canon and so declared to be." (James M. Gray, *Primers of the Faith*, p.2)

The Bible's authority for faith and practice rises from its origin. Its writers referred to it as "Holy Scriptures" (<u>Rom. 1:2</u>), or "sacred writings" (<u>2 Tim. 3:15</u>) and "the oracles of God" (<u>Heb. 5:12</u>).

The uniqueness of the Scriptures is based on their origin and source. The writers claimed they did not originate their messages but received them from the Holy Spirit of God. David said, "The Spirit of the Lord spoke to me, and His word was on my tongue" (2 Sam. 23:2).

The New Testament recognized the role of the Holy Spirit in the production of the Old Testament. Jesus said David was inspired by the Holy Spirit (Mark 12:36). Paul believed the Holy Spirit spoke "through Isaiah" (Acts 28:25). Peter stated the Holy Spirit guided all the prophets, not just a few (1 Pet. 1:10-11; 2 Pet. 1:21).

The New Testament writers also recognized the Holy Spirit as the source of their own messages.

So God, in the person of the Holy Spirit, has revealed Himself through the Holy Scriptures. And since God the Holy Spirit inspired the writers, God, then, is its author.

Reasons for the truthfulness and inspiration of Scripture are numerous. Let me list just a few:

1. The Argument from the Indestructibility of the Bible.

Only a small percentage of books survive even a century and a very small number continue over a thousand years. Since the Bible is over 3,500 years running and continues to be published as the #1 seller of all history, it is a unique book. Then, when you consider the circumstances under which the Bible has survived, this fact becomes even more startling.

Following the founding of the Church, the Roman emperors soon discovered that the Christians grounded their beliefs on the Scriptures. Consequently, they sought to suppress or exterminate them. Diocletian, by a royal edict in 303 A.D., demanded that every copy of the Bible be destroyed by fire. He killed so many Christians and had so many Bibles destroyed that when the Christians went into hiding, he thought he had actually put an end to the Scriptures.

He even caused a medal to be struck with the inscription: "The Christian religion is destroyed and the worship of the gods restored."

But just a few years later Constantine came to the throne and he made Christianity the state religion of Rome.

During the **Reformation**, the Roman Catholic Church resisted the Bible being translated into the tongue of the common people and set up severe restrictions on the grounds that the common person was incapable of interpreting it.

In 1543, an act was passed forbidding the use of Tyndale's version or any reading of the Scriptures in assemblies without royal license. Of the estimated 18,000 copies of Tyndale's translation printed between 1525-1528, only two fragments are known to remain.

However, neither imperial edict, nor papal restraint, and centuries of persecution have succeeded in exterminating the Bible.

2. The Argument from the <u>Character</u> of the Bible

When honestly looking at the character of the Bible you are forced to come to but one conclusion: It is the embodiment of a divine revelation.

a. Because of its **Contents**. The Bible recognizes throughout its pages, the personality, unity, and trinity of God. It magnifies the holiness and love of God; it accounts for the creation of man made in the image of God; it represents the fall of man as a free revolt against the revealed will of God; it pictures sin as inexcusable and under eternal judgment; it teaches the sovereign rule of God; it sets forth God's provision of salvation; it delineates the purposes of God for Israel and the Church; it forecasts the developments of the world, society, economically, politically, and religiously; it portrays the culmination of all things in the second coming of Christ. What a book! Who, but God, could have thought up such a scheme and who but He could have reduced it to writing.

b. Because of the **Unity** of the Bible. Unlike the Koran or the book of Mormon, which were written by one person and yet contain contradictory statements, the Bible was written by some forty different authors over a period of about 1500 years and remains one book with one doctrinal system, one moral standard, one plan of salvation, and one program for the ages.

Its several accounts of the same incidents or teachings are not contradictory, but supplementary. For example, the superscription on the Cross was as follows:

"This is Jesus of Nazareth, the King of the Jews."

Matthew – "This is the King of the Jews" (Matt. 27:37)
Mark – "The King of the Jews" (Mark 15:26)
Luke – "This is the King of the Jews" (Luke 23:38)
John – "Jesus of Nazareth, the King of the Jews" (John 19:19)

Law and grace perfectly harmonize when we understand the exact nature and purpose of each.

3. The Argument Regarding the Influence of the Bible

When you compare the influence of writings like: the Koran, the Book of Mormon, Science and Health, the Hindu Vedas, the teachings of Buddha, the Classics of Confucius, etc. with the kind of influence the Bible has had on the world, it is entirely different.

Not only has the Bible brought an intimate knowledge of God to man, but it produces amazing transformation in the lives of those who put their trust in Jesus; releasing the highest levels of creativity in the field of arts, architecture, literature, medicine, and music.

Think of the great paintings of Michelangelo, Leonardo da Vinci, and the Dutch masters. Envision the great cathedrals in Europe and America; recall the great hymns, psalms and spiritual songs of the church; and examine the great social reforms made by freeing the slaves, and recognizing the rights of women; in addition to the numerous medical breakthroughs and the thousands of hospitals established around the world by missionaries.

Where is there a book, in all the world, that even remotely compares with the Bible in its beneficial influence upon mankind?

4. The Argument from Fulfilled Prophecies

Isaiah 42:9 – *"Everything I prophesied has come true, and now I will prophesy again. I will tell you the future before it happens."* (NLT)

Isaiah 44:7 – *"Who else can tell you what is going to happen in the days ahead? Let them tell you if they can and thus prove their power. Let them do as I have done since ancient times."* (NLT)

Isa. 43:9 – *"Gather the nations together! Which of their idols has ever foretold such things? Can any of them predict something even a single day in advance? Where are the witnesses of such predictions? Who can verify that they spoke the truth?"* (NLT)

Isaiah 46:9-10 – *"And do not forget the things I have done throughout history. For I am God—I alone! I am God, and there is no one else like me. Only I can tell you what is going to happen even before it happens. Everything I plan will come to pass, for I do whatever I wish."* (NLT)

Only God can reveal the future, and we have many proofs in the Bible that He did reveal the future to His servants. There are numerous predictive prophecies concerning Christ (hundreds of years before his coming), which were fulfilled when He came.

The prophecies concerning Israel's dispersion were fulfilled in detail. Samaria would be overthrown, but Judah preserved (Isa. 7:6-8; Hosea 1:6-7; 1 Kings 14:15). Judah and Jerusalem were to be rescued from the Assyrians, but would fall into the hands of the Babylonians (Isa. 39:6; Jer. 25:9-12).

Prophecies concerning the Gentile nations of Nineveh, Babylon, Tyre, Egypt, Ammon, Moab, Edom, and Philistia can all be located with an exhaustive concordance.

Then there are many Bible prophecies being fulfilled in our day. Daniel's image, depicting human government concludes with the ten toes made up of iron mixed with clay. Most of Daniel's vision has already come to pass, but now I believe the last part of his vision is being fulfilled in the transitions within the middle East nations. (Dan. 2, 7).

As prophesied by Ezekiel, we're seeing the restoration of the nation of Israel and the return of the Jews to their homeland after almost 2000 years (Rom. 11:25-32)(Ezek. 37:1-28). We're also seeing the increase of wars and rumors of wars (Matt. 24:6-7); the increased number and severity of earthquakes and famines; the increase of knowledge and worldwide travel (2 Tim. 3:7); and the increase of lawlessness and wickedness (Matt. 24:12).

All have been prophesied in Scripture and are presently being fulfilled before our eyes.

IV. The WORD – God's Basis For Judgment

1 Samuel 5:1-12 – *"Then the Philistines took the ark of God and brought it from Ebenezer to Ashdod. When the Philistines took the ark of God, they brought it into the house of Dagon and set it by Dagon. And when the people of Ashdod arose early in the morning, there was Dagon, fallen on its face to the earth before the ark of the LORD. So they took Dagon and set it in its place again. And when they arose early the next morning, there was Dagon, fallen on its face to the ground before the ark of the LORD. The head of Dagon and both the palms of its hands were broken off on the threshold; only Dagon's torso was left of it. Therefore neither the priests of Dagon nor any who come into Dagon's house tread on the threshold of Dagon in Ashdod to this day.*

*But the hand of the LORD was heavy on the people of **Ashdod**, and He ravaged them and struck them with tumors, both Ashdod and its territory. And when the men of Ashdod saw how it was, they said, 'The ark of the God of Israel must not remain with us, for His hand is harsh toward us and Dagon our god.' Therefore they sent and gathered to themselves all the lords of the Philistines, and said, 'What shall we do with the ark of the God of Israel?'*

*And they answered, 'Let the ark of the God of Israel be carried away to **Gath**.' So they carried the ark of the God of Israel away. So it was, after they had carried it away, that the hand of the LORD was against the city with a very great destruction; and He struck the men of the city, both small and great, and tumors broke out on them.*

*Therefore they sent the ark of God to **Ekron**. So it was, as the ark of God came to Ekron, that the Ekronites cried out, saying, "They have brought the ark of the God of Israel to us, to kill us and our people!" So they sent and gathered together all the lords of the Philistines, and said, 'Send away the ark of the God of Israel, and let it go back to its own place, so that it does not kill us and our people.' For there was a deadly destruction throughout all the city; the hand of God was very heavy there. And the men who did not die were stricken with the tumors, and the cry of the city went up to heaven."* (NKJV)

Ashdod meaning "stronghold, fortress", is one of the five ruling cities of the Philistines. The others are Gaza, Ashkelon, Gath and Ekron.

Ashdod was the center for Dagon (fish-god) worship, and believing that Dagon had enabled them to win the battle against Israel, the Ark of Yahweh was brought and placed before the idol Dagon as the choice piece of the spoil taken from the battlefield. It was a major prize, if you will.

The Philistines were gloating over their victory just as non-believers gloat over their perceived victory over God's Word in the present day.

However, Jesus, the Word of the living God, judges all people, nations, and cultures.

Eph. 1:20-22 – *"That power… which he exerted in Christ when he raised him from the dead and seated him at his right hand in the heavenly realms, far above all rule and authority, power and dominion, and every title that can be given, not only in the present age but also in the one to come. And God placed all things under his feet and appointed him to be head over everything for the church."* (NIV)

Phil. 2:9-10 – *"Therefore God exalted him to the highest place and gave him the name that is above every name, that at the name of Jesus every knee should bow, in heaven and on earth and under the earth."* (NIV)

John 5:22 – *"In addition, the Father judges no one. Instead, he has given the Son absolute authority to judge."*

John 12:48 – *"There is a judge for the one who rejects me and does not accept my words; that very word which I spoke will condemn him at the last day."* (NIV)

John 5:22, 26-27 – *"And the Father leaves all judgment to his Son … The Father has life in himself, and he has granted his Son to have life in himself. And he has given him authority to judge all mankind because he is the Son of Man."*

Acts 10:42 – *"God told us to announce clearly to the people that Jesus is the one he has chosen to judge the living and the dead."* (CEV)

Acts 17:31 – *"God has set a day that he will judge all the world with fairness, by the man he chose long ago. And God has proved this to everyone by raising that man from the dead!"* (CEV)

Jesus, the living and eternal Word of the Almighty God, has been given the authority to judge individuals, cities, and nations in all situations and at all times. Nothing is outside the realm of accountability to Him.

And just as he exercised his authority amongst the Philistines, he can and does exercise his authority amongst the nations today.

No earthly governmental power or false religion will escape accountability to Him.

Jesus is Lord!

The admonition of Scripture, for everyone who calls himself a Christian, is to make Jesus Christ the Lord of your life. Make Him Lord over what you think, speak, and do.

Col. 2:6-10 – *"And now, just as you accepted Christ Jesus as your Lord, you must continue to follow him. Let your roots grow down into him, and let your lives be built on him. Then your faith will grow strong in the truth you were taught, and you will overflow with thankfulness. Don't let anyone capture you with empty philosophies and high-sounding nonsense that come from human thinking and from the spiritual powers of this world, rather than from Christ. For in Christ lives all the fullness of God in a human body. So you also are complete through your union with Christ, who is the head over every ruler and authority."*

V. The WORD – Ultimately Triumphant

1 Sam. 6:1-21 – *"The ark of the Lord was in the country of the Philistines **seven** months. And the Philistines called for the priests and the diviners and said, 'What shall we do with the ark of the Lord? Tell us how we should send it to its place.' They said, 'If you send away the ark of the God of Israel, do not send it empty; but by all means return Him a guilt offering. Then you will be healed, and it will be known to you why His hand does not turn away from you.' And they said, 'What is the guilt offering that we shall return to Him?' They answered, 'Five golden tumors and five golden mice, according* *to the number of the lords of the Philistines, for the same plague was on all of you and on your lords. So you must make images of your tumors and images of your mice that ravage the land, and give glory to the God of Israel. Perhaps He will lighten His hand from off you and your gods and your land. Why should you harden your hearts as the Egyptians and Pharaoh hardened their hearts? After He had dealt severely with them, did they not send the people away, and they departed? Now then, take and prepare a new cart and two milk cows on which there has never been a yoke, and yoke the cows to the cart, but take their calves home, away from them. And take the ark of the Lord and place it on the cart and put in a box at its side the figures of gold, which you are returning to Him as a guilt offering. Then send it off and let it go its way and watch. If it goes up on the way to its own land, to Beth-shemesh, then it is He who has done us this great harm, but if not, then we shall know that it is not His hand that struck us; it happened to us by coincidence.'*

Then the men did so and took two milk cows and yoked them to the cart and shut up their calves at home. And they put the ark of the Lord on the cart and the box with the golden mice and the images of their tumors. And the cows went straight in the direction of Beth-shemesh, along one highway, lowing as they went. They turned neither to the right hand or the left, and the lords of the Philistines went after them as far as the border of Beth-shemesh. Now the people of Beth-shemesh were reaping their wheat harvest in the valley. And when they lifted their eyes and saw the ark, they rejoiced to see it. The cart came into the field of Joshua of Beth-shemesh and stopped there. A great stone was there. And they split up the wood of the cart and offered the cows as a burnt offering to the Lord. And the Levites took down the ark of the Lord and the box that was beside it, in which were the golden figures, and set them upon the great stone. And the men of Beth-shemesh offered burnt offerings and made sacrifices on that day to the Lord. And when the five lords of the Philistines saw it, they returned that day to Ekron.

These are the golden tumors that the Philistines returned as a guilt offering to the Lord: one for Ashdod, one for Gaza, one for Ashkelon, one for Gath, one for Ekron; and the golden mice, according to the number of all the cities of the Philistines belonging to the five lords, both fortified cities and unwalled villages. The great stone beside which they set down the ark of the Lord is a witness to this day in the field of Joshua of Beth-shemesh.

And He struck some of the men of Beth-shemesh, because they had looked into the ark of the Lord. He struck seventy men of them, and the people mourned because the Lord had struck the people with a great blow. Then the men of Beth-shemesh said, 'Who is able to stand before the Lord, this holy God? And to whom shall he go up away from us?' So they sent messengers to the inhabitants of Kirjath Jearim, saying, "The Philistines have returned the ark of the Lord. Come down and take it up to you.' " (ESV)

When the Israelites were initially defeated by the Philistines, it should have been sufficient evidence for them to know that God was displeased with them. But, did they repent and turn to God in prayer and confession? No!

Instead, they took action according to the superstitious wisdom of the world and took the Ark of God into the battlefield, hoping that somehow it would save them.

To take the Ark into battle was not an act of faith. How do we know it was not an act of faith? We know, because God had not commanded them by his Word.

Biblical faith requires two important factors: **1)** It requires that the Word of God, whether it comes by dream, vision, audible voice or Holy Scriptures, be made alive and spoken into the human spirit, by the Holy Spirit. **2)** It also requires the exercise of one's personal capacity to believe, expressed in trusting action.

VI. The Reason For God's Judgment

Now, although God refused to act on behalf of His sinful and unbelieving people and allowed the Ark of His presence to be momentarily taken captive, He would not allow His glory to be mocked by a smirking enemy.

The first day the Ark was placed in the Temple of Dagon, Yahweh gave the Philistines a clear message of who was the real God. Early in the morning, the priests find the idol of the phony god fallen, face down before the Ark; and on the second morning, it is once again fallen face down before the Ark, plus its head and hands are removed and lying on the threshold.

In this action, Yahweh proves Dagon to be a false man-made god.

Over and over again, down through the centuries, the godless and unbelieving have endeavored to prove the Bible as unreliable or incorrect in its historical data. And over and over again, God has proven the unbelieving wrong through subsequent archeological findings.

As Judge of all the earth, God not only confronts the vain religious philosophies of the world, He also confronts its nations, tribes, or various peoples groups for living in sin. He doesn't do this arbitrarily. In fact, the land of Canaan was deeded by the Creator to the descendents of Abraham, Isaac and Jacob, but they had to wait 400 years until the cup of iniquity was filled by these sinful nations.

Gen. 15:13-16 – *"The Lord said to him, 'Your descendants will be strangers in a foreign land; they will be slaves there and will be treated cruelly for four hundred years. But I will punish the nation that enslaves them, and when they leave that foreign land, they will take great wealth with them. You yourself will live to a ripe old age, die in peace, and be buried. It will be four generations before your descendants come back here, because I will not drive out the Amorites until they become so wicked that they must be punished.'"* (TEV)

God's judgment in the case of Adam and Eve, and all down through history is a clear revelation that God is holy and His Word is holy. God's holiness requires that He cannot abide sin. His justice demands that He deal with it.

So, His divine redemptive provision, until the sacrifice of Messiah, was the sacrificial worship of Israel, which provided, from year to year, the blood covering for the sins of the people; that alone kept God's holiness from utterly destroying them.

Exodus 33:1-3 – *"Then the Lord said to Moses, 'Leave this place, you and the people you brought up out of Egypt, and go up to the land I promised on oath to Abraham, Isaac and Jacob, saying, I will give it to your descendants.' I will send an angel before you and drive out the Canaanites, Amorites, Hittites, Perizzites, Hivites and Jebusites. Go up to the land flowing with milk and honey. But I will not go with you, because you are a stiff-necked people and I might destroy you on the way.'"* (NIV)

VII. God's Judgments Will Ultimately Accomplish God's Purpose

1 Samuel 6:1 – *"The Ark of the Lord remained in Philistine territory seven months in all."* (NLT)

The Ark of God appeared to be a captive prize of war. However, appearances can be deceiving.

The number seven, in this passage, represents a significant number, because it took only **seven months**, under the hand of Yahweh, for the Philistines to get the message that the God of the Israelites is the sovereign Judge over the nations.

Now, during the Great Tribulation, God will test and try the whole earth for a **seven-year** period. During the last 3½ years, men will cry for the mountains to fall on them because His wrath is being poured out on the earth.

Seven is a number in the Bible that represents completeness, maturity or perfection.

Jer. 10:10-11 – *"But the Lord is the only true God, the living God. He is the everlasting King! The whole earth trembles at his anger. The nations hide before his wrath. Say this to those who worship other gods: 'Your so-called gods, who did not make the heavens and earth, will vanish from the earth.'"*

Zeph. 1:14-15 – *"That terrible day of the Lord is near. Swiftly it comes—a day when strong men will cry bitterly. It is a day when the Lord's anger will be poured out. It is a day of terrible distress and anguish, a day of ruin and desolation, a day of darkness and gloom, of clouds, blackness."*

Rev. 6:16-17 – *"They called to the mountains and the rocks, 'Fall on us and hide us from the face of him who sits on the throne and from the wrath of the Lamb! For the great day of their wrath has come, and who can stand?'"* (NIV)

Rev. 19:13-16 – *"He was clothed with a robe dipped in blood, and his title was the Word of God. The armies of heaven, dressed in pure white linen, followed him on white horses. From his mouth came a sharp sword, and with it he struck down the nations. He ruled them with an iron rod, and he trod the winepress of the fierce wrath of almighty God. On his robe and thigh was written this title: King of kings and Lord of lords."*

Jesus is the living Word of God and he is the same yesterday, today, and forever. God always was the Judge, He is the Judge, and He will always be the Judge and His judgment is true.

The pagan priests advised the leaders, "If the plague was to be removed, an acknowledgment of guilt was needed and a guilt offering should be sent along with the Ark as reparation to appease the God whose anger had been unleashed against them."

The guilt offering was to consist of 5 golden "tumors" and 5 golden mice, in the likeness of the mice that ravished the land. In this way they would be giving glory to God and making it possible for Him to withdraw His hand from them.

To determine whether their national misfortune was simply a natural disaster, or whether it was due to the judgment of God, two milk cows were separated from their calves and hitched to a new cart which had not been defiled by common labor.

The Ark was placed on the cart drawn by these two milk cows, along with a chest containing the guilt offering of molded golden tumors and mice. Now, the lords of the Philistines followed the cart to guarantee that no one would tamper with their experiment.

Rather than turn back to their calves, the cows went straight down the road to Beth-Shemesh lowing as they went, under divine compulsion. They turned neither to the right nor to the left.

This unnatural behavior of the cows convinced the Philistines that the disaster was not mere chance. Truly, the hand of Yahweh had smitten the Philistines. Ironically, the test simply gave the Lord another opportunity to demonstrate his power.

Now the farmers of the village of Beth-Shemesh rejoiced when they saw the Ark. The cows stopped near a large stone in the field of one named Joshua. The Levites removed the Ark and placed it on the large stone. A fire was built with the wood of the cart and the cows were slaughtered and offered to God as a burnt offering. Other sacrifices apparently were also offered.

From a distance the lords of the Philistines looked on as the chest containing their guilt offering was opened. There the Israelites found the golden mice and five golden tumors. The large stone where the Ark had been placed became a kind of national monument, a witness to the day when the Ark came home.

At this point, the Biblical narrative takes a surprising turn. In their exuberance over the return of the Ark, the men of Beth-Shemesh made a serious mistake. They looked inside the Ark.

Their motives may have been prompted by simple curiosity. They probably wished to see if the Philistines had removed any of the memorial objects, which were contained in the Ark.

Nonetheless, looking into the Ark with profane curiosity was strictly forbidden. So the Lord smote the people of Beth-Shemesh with a great slaughter and the leaders of Beth-Shemesh quickly sent to Kiriath-jearim to ask them to come and take away the Ark.

The Levites from Kiriath-jearim were much more knowledgeable about how to properly care for the Ark of God.

Numbers 4:18-20 – *"See that the Kohathite tribal clans are not cut off from the Levites. So that they may live and not die when they come near the most holy things, do this for them: Aaron and his sons are to go into the sanctuary and assign to each man his work and what he is to carry. But the Kohathites must not go in to look at the holy things, even for a moment, or they will die."* (NIV)

The number of people affected by the plague at Beth-shemesh is in dispute. Actually the Hebrew text contains two numbers side by side, seventy and fifty thousand. All of the most recent translations, such as the NIV, NLT, NJB, NCV, TEV, CEV, and the LB chose the smaller figure, regarding the fifty thousand as an error in translation.

The Critical and Explanatory Commentary on the Old Testament, by Jamieson, Fausset, and Brown states: "Beth-Shemesh being only a village, this translation *must* be erroneous, and should be, "he smote fifty out of a thousand," being only fourteen hundred in all who indulged this curiosity. God, instead of decimating, according to an ancient usage, slew only a twentieth part; that is, according to JOSEPHUS, seventy out of fourteen hundred" (see <u>Num. 4:18–22</u>).[8]

---

[8]   Jamieson, R., Fausset, A. R., Fausset, A. R., Brown, D., & Brown, D. 1997. *A commentary, critical and explanatory, on the Old and New Testaments*. On

It is a great affront to God, for individuals to pry into and meddle with the secret things, which do not belong to them. Adam brought the entire human race under God's condemnation by rejecting God's Word and desiring forbidden knowledge.

God will not suffer his Word or His presence to be profaned.

Be not deceived, God is not mocked. Any person that does not fear the Lord and reverently humble himself or herself in submission to His Word shall be made to experience his justice.

Deut. 29:29 – *"Some things are hidden. They belong to the Lord our God. But the things that have been revealed in these teachings belong to us and to our children forever. We must obey every word of these teachings."* (GW)

I believe God wants us to gain certain insights from this passage of Scripture concerning His will for us. First of all, we need to be mindful that His Word has never lost its power and in these last days, His Word will surely judge the nations.

If we approach our study of God's Word and look into it with prideful and arrogant curiosity, it will only produce spiritual death in us. But if we humbly ask the Holy Spirit to reveal the things of God to us, we will benefit from all its hidden treasures.

Even though portions of the Church may fail to walk in righteousness, as Hophni and Phinehas failed, and may fail to properly handle God's Word, as in the case of using it as a fetish to try to win a battle with the enemy, God remains faithful and He will raise up a faithful priesthood who will do all that is in His heart and mind.

We must believe the Word of the Lord!!!!

In the next chapter we will see that God uses His life-giving eternal Word to deliver us from the domination of our sin nature and through the consecration of our lives, He restores us to fellowship with Himself.

---

spine: Critical and explanatory commentary. Logos Research Systems, Inc.: Oak Harbor, WA

Psalm 32:1-11

A psalm of David.
Oh, what joy for those whose rebellion is forgiven, whose sin is put out of sight!
[2] Yes, what joy for those whose record the Lord has cleared of sin, whose lives are lived in complete honesty!

[3] When I refused to confess my sin, I was weak and miserable, and I groaned all day long.
[4] Day and night your hand of discipline was heavy on me.
My strength evaporated like water in the summer heat. *Interlude*

[5] Finally, I confessed all my sins to you and stopped trying to hide them.
I said to myself, "I will confess my rebellion to the Lord."
And you forgave me! All my guilt is gone. *Interlude*

[6] Therefore, let all the godly confess their rebellion to you while there is time,
that they may not drown in the floodwaters of judgment.
[7] For you are my hiding place; you protect me from trouble.
You surround me with songs of victory. *Interlude*

[8] The Lord says, "I will guide you along the best pathway for your life.
I will advise you and watch over you.
[9] Do not be like a senseless horse or mule
that needs a bit and bridle to keep it under control."

[10] Many sorrows come to the wicked, but unfailing love surrounds those who trust the Lord.
[11] So rejoice in the Lord and be glad, all you who obey him!
Shout for joy, all you whose hearts are pure! (NLT)

CHAPTER TWELVE

The Restorative Power of God's Word

1 Sam. 7:1-6 – *"Then the men of Kiriath-jearim came and took the ark of the LORD, and brought it into the house of Abinadab on the hill, and* **consecrated Eleazar** *his son to keep the ark of the LORD. So it was that the ark remained in Kiriath-jearim a long time; it was there twenty years. And all the house of Israel* **lamented** *after the LORD. Then Samuel spoke to all the house of Israel, saying, 'If you* **return** *to the LORD with all your hearts, then* **put away** *the* **foreign gods** *and the* **Ashtoreths** *from among you, and* **prepare your hearts** *for the LORD, and* **serve Him only***; and He will deliver you from the hand of the Philistines.' So the children of Israel put away the* **Baals** *and the* **Ashtoreths***, and served the LORD only.*

*And Samuel said, '***Gather all** *Israel to* **Mizpah***, and I will pray to the LORD for you.' So they gathered together at Mizpah,* **drew** *water, and* **poured it out** *before the LORD. And they* **fasted** *that day, and said there, 'We have sinned against the LORD.' And Samuel judged the children of Israel at Mizpah."* (NKJV)

Trusting in ourselves and leaning on our own understanding, as Israel did, will always bring us to a crisis experience where the Lord seeks to deliver us from trusting in the arm of the flesh. Once we lose confidence in our own wisdom and abilities, as a result of experiencing defeat at the hand of our enemies, we must return to the Lord with all our heart.

Hosea 6:1-3 – *"Come, let us return to the Lord. He has torn us to pieces but he will heal us; he has injured us but he will bind up our wounds. After two days he will revive us; on the third day he will* restore *us, that we may live in his presence. Let us acknowledge the Lord; let us press on to* *acknowledge him. As surely as the sun rises, he will appear; he will come to us like the winter rains, like the spring rains that water the earth." (NIV)*

Joel 2:12-13 – *"'Even now', declares the Lord, 'return to me with all your heart, with fasting and weeping and mourning. Rend your heart and not your garments.' Return to the Lord your God, for he is gracious and compassionate, slow to anger and abounding in love, and he relents from sending calamity." (NIV)*

Isaiah 55:7 – *"Let the people turn from their wicked deeds. Let them banish from their minds the very thought of doing wrong! Let them turn to the Lord that he may have mercy on them. Yes, turn to our God, for he will abundantly pardon." (NLT)*

Deut. 30:2-10 – *"… when you and your children **return** to the Lord your God and obey him with all your heart and with all your soul according to everything I command you today, then the Lord your God will **restore your fortunes** and **have compassion on you** and gather you again from all the nations where he scattered you. Even if you have been banished to the most distant land under the heavens, from there the Lord your God will gather you and bring you back. He will bring you to the land that belonged to your fathers, and you will take possession of it. He will make you **more prosperous** and **numerous** than your fathers. The Lord your God will **circumcise your hearts** and the hearts of your descendants, so that you may love him with all your heart and with all your soul, and live. The Lord your God will **put all these curses on your enemies** who hate and persecute you. You will again obey the Lord and follow all his commands I am giving you today. Then the Lord your **God will make you most prosperous** in all the work of your hands and in the fruit of your womb, the young of your livestock and the crops of your land. The Lord will again **delight in you** and **make you prosperous**, just as he delighted in your fathers, if you obey the Lord your God and keep his commands and decrees that are written in this Book of the Law and turn to the Lord your God with all your heart and with all your soul." (NIV)*

The **purpose** in **returning to the Lord** is to **obey** him with all your heart and with all your soul according to his commands, or the Word of the Lord. The **reason** or **motivation** for returning to the Lord is to receive His **healing** and **blessing**.

If you are tired of living your life without God's blessing and there are still areas of your life that are ruled over by your flesh or they contain enemy strongholds, I would urge you to return to the Lord your God. Return to him this day with all your heart and with all your soul.

I. Consecration – Necessary to Properly Care for the Ark of His Presence

The proper care of the Ark or the handling of God's Word and the ability to return to the Lord with all your heart and soul, begins with consecrating yourself to serve Him only.

Rom. 12:1 – *"I appeal to you therefore, brethren, and beg of you in view of [all] the mercies of God, to make a decisive dedication of your bodies [presenting all your members and faculties] as a living sacrifice, holy (devoted, consecrated) and well pleasing to God, which is your reasonable (rational, intelligent) service and spiritual worship."* (Amp)

To **consecrate** is to: induct a person into a permanent office; to devote irrevocably to the worship of God; to be dedicated to a sacred purpose. Eleazar was consecrated and permanently set apart for the worshipful and sacred care of the Ark.

Anything that is consecrated or declared "holy" is set apart and removed from the realm of the common and moved to the sphere of the sacred.

For instance: the seventh day of creation was consecrated by God and declared "holy." It was set aside and reserved for worship and rest. God sanctified Mount Sinai when He appeared there and gave Moses the Ten Commandments. Aaron's family and the Levitical priests were made holy when they were consecrated to God's service of worship.

We can better understand the importance of consecration and properly preparing ourselves to meet with God when we read:

2 Chron. 30:17-20 – *"Since many people in the crowd had not made themselves holy, the Levites killed the Passover lambs for everyone who was not clean. The Levites made each lamb holy for the Lord. Although many people from Ephraim, Manasseh, Issachar, and Zebulun had not purified themselves for the feast, they ate the Passover even though it was against* *the law. So Hezekiah prayed for them, saying, 'Lord, you are good. You are the Lord, the God of our ancestors. Please forgive all those who try to obey you even if they did not make themselves clean as the rules of the Temple command.' The Lord listened to Hezekiah's prayer, and he healed the people."* (NCV)

Healing the people became a necessity, because God had already begun judging them for not consecrating themselves and properly preparing to feast in His presence.

Being set apart and dedicated for a ministry ordained by God is necessary to establish a proper mental attitude toward handling the Word of God. That includes any ministry that is involved in communicating the Word of God to others.

Consecration to serve the Lord requires making a meaningful choice as Joshua did.

Joshua 24:14-15 – *"Now fear the Lord and serve him with all faithfulness. Throw away the gods your forefathers worshiped beyond the River and in Egypt, and serve the Lord. But if serving the Lord seems undesirable to you, then choose for yourselves this day whom you will serve, whether the gods your forefathers served beyond the River, or the gods of the Amorites, in whose land you are living. But as for me and my household, we will serve the Lord."* (NIV)

II. The Necessary Preparation of the Heart

Properly preparing your heart to return to the Lord includes:

1. **Lamentation** – "to make ritualized motions and sounds of sorrow, as an act of repentance, implying a change of behavior."

Israel **mourned** or **lamented** for Yahweh for 20 years. This passage, as well as life experience, teaches us that God is not to be trifled with or treated as though you can enter and withdraw from His presence any time you choose.

If we are careless about sinning, God will withdraw the conscious awareness of His presence in order to make you ultimately desire Him and He won't give you back that awareness of His presence until you have truly repented.

2. Put Away the Baals and Ashtoreths

Baal – Name of the most prominent Canaanite deity. As the god of fertility in the Canaanite pantheon (roster of gods), Baal's sphere of influence included agriculture, animal husbandry, and human sexuality.[9]

Asherah – a Canaanite goddess of fertility, the wife of El according to Ugaritic tradition, but the consort of Baal in Palestine. In the Ugaritic literature she is called 'Lady Asherah of the Sea,' a title that may signify 'she who treads on the sea.'

Apart from her name, she has other connections with the sea. Her servant is called 'fisherman of Lady Asherah of the Sea.' [10]

Now, Asherah can also refer to a cult object or objects. So, the command to "put away these gods" meant that the people of Israel were to reject not only the practices of these religions, but they were to get rid of any idols or fetishes connected with these religions.

These gods not only represented certain aspects and powers of nature, but there were philosophies and religious practices associated with the worship of these gods that were strictly forbidden by Yahweh. Forbidden, not just because they presented false ideas of reality, but also because they produced a society that would be given over to immorality and violence.

3. Gather All Israel to Mizpah

Eph. 2:6 – *"And God raised us up with Christ and seated us with him in the heavenly realms in Christ Jesus."* (NIV)

Why do we need to gather to Mizpah?

Mizpah – A high tower; a watchtower lookout post.

---

[9] Elwell, W. A., & Beitzel, B. J. 1988. *Baker encyclopedia of the Bible*. Map on lining papers. Baker Book House: Grand Rapids, Mich.

[10] Achtemeier, P. J., Harper & Row, P., & Society of Biblical Literature. 1985. *Harper's Bible dictionary*. Includes index. (1st ed.). Harper & Row: San Francisco

Serving false, manmade gods leaves us with a worldly self-centered perspective on life. And like Israel of old, every believer needs their mind renewed with the Word of God.

Israel needed to change their perspective. They needed to start seeing from a heavenly perspective. In the same way, we need to realize that God has raised us up and seated us in heavenly places in Christ for a reason.

He has done that so we could begin to observe life and understand life's experiences from a heavenly or Biblical perspective.

Endeavoring to observe life from any other perspective than God's makes us susceptible to deception and definitely limited to a worldly or secular view.

4. Draw Water and Pour It Out Before the Lord

The drink offering was required with all freewill and consecratory offerings. So, when Jacob encountered God at Bethel, he consecrated the stone as a memorial of his encounter with God.

Genesis 35:14 – *"Jacob set up a stone on edge in that place where God had talked to him, and he poured a drink offering and olive oil on it to make it special for God."* (NCV)

The drink offering is also a type of Christ pouring out his life for us. So, the act of consecrating our life to do the will of God also includes identifying with Christ in a willingness to pour out our lives in love for others.

Psalm 22:14 – *"My life is poured out like water, and all my bones are out of joint. My heart is like wax, melting within me."* (NLT)

Isaiah prophesied concerning Christ's death on the cross, saying:

Isaiah 53:12 – *"Therefore I will give him a portion among the great, and he will divide the spoils with the strong, because **he poured out his life unto death**, and was numbered with the transgressors. For he bore the sin of many, and made intercession for the transgressors."* (NIV)

2 Sam. 23:15-17 – *"David longed for water and said, 'Oh, that someone would get me a drink of water from the well near the gate of Bethlehem!' So the three mighty men broke through the Philistine lines, drew water from* the well near the gate of Bethlehem and carried it back to David. But he refused to drink it; instead, he poured it out before the Lord. 'Far be it from me, O Lord, to do this!' he said. 'Is it not the blood of men who went **at the risk of their lives**?' And David would not drink it. Such were the exploits of the three mighty men." (NIV)

Jesus said, *"If you try to keep your life for yourself, you will lose it. But if you give up your life for my sake and for the sake of the Good News, you will find true life."* **Mark 8:35**

Paul embraced this truth of consecration and applied it to his own life; and in addition, he passed it on to those who worked with him.

Acts 20:24 – *"But my life is worth nothing unless I use it for doing the work assigned me by the Lord Jesus—the work of telling others the Good News about God's wonderful kindness and love."* (NLT)

Romans 16:3-4 – *"Greet Priscilla and Aquila. They have been co-workers in my ministry for Christ Jesus. In fact, **they risked their lives** for me. I am not the only one who is thankful to them; so are all the Gentile churches."* (NLT)

Phil. 2:25-30 – *"Meanwhile, I thought I should send Epaphroditus back to you. He is a true brother, a faithful worker, and a courageous soldier... For **he risked his life for the work of Christ**, and he was at the point of death while trying to do for me the things you couldn't do because you were far away."* (NLT)

5. They Fasted on that Day

Prayer and fasting is supposed to be a consistent part of our walk with God. It is a proper way of humbling ourselves so that we come before the Lord in true sincerity of heart.

Daniel gives us a wonderful example as he cried out to God on behalf of himself and his fellow Israelites.

Daniel 9:3-19 – *"So I turned to the Lord God and pleaded with him **in prayer and fasting**. I wore rough sackcloth and sprinkled myself with ashes. I prayed to the Lord my God and confessed: 'O Lord, you are a great and awesome God! You always fulfill your promises of unfailing love to those who love you and keep your commands. But we have sinned and done wrong.*

We have rebelled against you and scorned your commands and regulations. We have refused to listen to your servants the prophets, who spoke your messages to our kings and princes and ancestors and to all the people of the land.

'Lord, you are in the right; but our faces are covered with shame, just as you see us now. This is true of us all, including the people of Judah and Jerusalem and all Israel, scattered near and far, wherever you have driven us because of our disloyalty to you. O Lord, we and our kings, princes, and ancestors are covered with shame because we have sinned against you. But the Lord our God is merciful and forgiving, even though we have rebelled against him. We have not obeyed the Lord our God, for we have not followed the laws he gave us through his servants the prophets. All Israel has disobeyed your law and turned away, refusing to listen to your voice.

'So now the solemn curses and judgments written in the Law of Moses, the servant of God, have been poured out against us because of our sin. You have done exactly what you warned you would do against us and our rulers. Never in all history has there been a disaster like the one that happened in Jerusalem. Every curse written against us in the Law of Moses has come true. All the troubles he predicted have taken place. But we have refused to seek mercy from the Lord our God by turning from our sins and recognizing his truth. The Lord has brought against us the disaster he prepared, for we did not obey him, and the Lord our God is just in everything he does.

'O Lord our God, you brought lasting honor to your name by rescuing your people from Egypt in a great display of power. But we have sinned and are full of wickedness. In view of all your faithful mercies, Lord, please turn your furious anger away from your city of Jerusalem, your holy mountain. All the neighboring nations mock Jerusalem and your people because of our sins and the sins of our ancestors.

'O our God, hear your servant's prayer! Listen as I plead. For your own sake, Lord, smile again on your desolate sanctuary.

'O my God, listen to me and hear my request. Open your eyes and see our wretchedness. See how your city lies in ruins—for everyone knows that it is yours. We do not ask because we deserve help, but because you are so merciful.

'O Lord, hear. O Lord, forgive. O Lord, listen and act! For your own sake, O my God, do not delay, for your people and your city bear your name.'" (NLT)

The passage of Scripture in first Samuel chapter seven, not only teaches how to return to the Lord as a nation, but also, how to draw near to God as individuals. We can walk out these truths and in so doing experience an abundant increase in God's blessing.

Returning to the Lord will require us to humble ourselves and put away the false gods erected by a corrupt, God-rejecting, western culture and world-system. It means casting down the human reasoning that is contrary to God's Word and purposing in our hearts to serve the Lord only.

We need to all gather to Mizpah and help each other relate to the 21st century with a heavenly perspective, with a Biblical Worldview.

We need to become victorious witnesses to the resurrection of Jesus, right where we live.

Overcoming the devil by the blood of the Lamb and by the Word contained in our bold testimony, and all the while not loving our lives, protecting, or coddling them; but instead, being willing to die for Christ's sake. (Rev. 12:11)

By returning to the Lord in humility and true repentance we are giving God the opportunity to revive us and grace us to live in the strength that comes from Christ alone.

Just as Paul testifies in his letter to the Galatians, by giving Jesus his rightful place as Lord in our life, we can live victoriously over our sin nature, of which Eli is a type (Gal.2:20).

CHAPTER THIRTEEN

The Necessity of Making Christ Preeminent

My mother has a definition of revival written inside the cover of her bible. It defines revival as: "The sovereign work of the Holy Spirit that brings the Church into a wonderful rediscovery of Jesus Christ, which, in turn, overthrows the status quo."

After twenty years of lamenting for the Lord God, the people of Israel are finally ready to hear the Word of the Lord through Samuel, the prophet. Samuel brings the Word of the Lord to all Israel saying, "If you return to the Lord with all your heart and soul, then put away the strange gods, prepare your hearts and serve the Lord only. Then, gather all Israel together at Mizpah and I will pray for you."

Preparing your heart to serve the Lord, through fasting and humble confession of sin, includes embracing an attitude of total abandonment to the will of God as seen in the drink offering. In other words, coming to the place mentally and emotionally of being willing to lay down your life for Christ's sake and the gospel's.

In essence, revival is freshly rediscovering Jesus Christ and giving him his rightful place in your life—seated on the throne of your heart.

The first step to experiencing personal revival is making:

I. Christ – The Rightful Lord of Your Life

1 Sam. 7:6 – *"And **Samuel judged** the children of Israel in Mizpah."* (NKJV)

Previously, **Eli** (a type of the flesh), as judge, was responsible to confront sinful behavior in Israel and motivate the Israelites to exhibit righteous behavior. And we know how good he was at doing that with his two sons Hophni and Phinehas.

At this point, **Samuel**, (a type of Christ) is the one judging and motivating Israel. A righteous judge, through the declaration of his righteous judgment, sets right what is wrong. And Christ, by the Holy Spirit, has taken up residence in your human spirit to do just that.

Rev. 1:12-18 – *"I turned around to see the voice that was speaking to me. And when I turned I saw seven golden lampstands, and among the lampstands was someone 'like a son of man,' dressed in a robe reaching down to his feet and with a golden sash around his chest. His head and hair were white like wool, as white as snow, and his eyes were like blazing fire. His feet were like bronze glowing in a furnace, and his voice was like the sound of rushing waters. In his right hand he held seven stars, and out of his mouth came a sharp double-edged sword. His face was like the sun shining in all its brilliance.*

When I saw him, I fell at his feet as though dead. Then he placed his right hand on me and said: 'Do not be afraid. I am the First and the Last. I am the Living One; I was dead, and behold I am alive forever and ever! And I hold the keys of death and Hades.'" (NIV)

Revelation 2:2 – *"**I know your deeds**, your hard work and your perseverance…"* (NIV)

When you read Christ's letters to the seven churches, you begin to understand that with eyes like blazing fire, there is no question as to why he is able to know the thoughts and intent of your heart. He can see into your very spirit and soul.

Do you think he has the authority and power to produce positive change in your life? To heal you and deliver you?

Jeremiah 17:9-10 – *"The human heart is most deceitful and desperately wicked. Who really knows how bad it is? But I know! I, the Lord, search* *all hearts and examine secret motives. I give all people their due rewards, according to what their actions deserve."*

Ezekiel 36:26 – *"And I will give you a new heart with new and right desires, and I will put a new spirit in you. I will take out your stony heart of sin and give you a new, obedient heart."*

Do you want Christ or your sin nature to sit on the throne of your life?

Once we humble ourselves in our desire to return to the Lord, by giving Christ His rightful place in our heart – which, by the way, requires of us the desire to gain a new perspective from God's Word – the enemy will hear about our newly embraced commitment to God and will attack in order to turn our hearts away from the Lord. It is a test of our commitment and our newly gained perspective of letting Christ rule and reign.

1 Sam. 7:7-10 – *"And **when the Philistines heard** that the children of Israel were gathered together to Mizpeh, the lords of the Philistines went up against Israel. And when the children of Israel heard it, **they were afraid** of the Philistines. And the children of Israel said to Samuel, **'Cease not to cry unto the LORD our God for us**, that he will save us out of the hand of the Philistines.' And **Samuel** took a sucking lamb, and **offered** it for **a burnt offering** wholly unto the LORD: and **Samuel cried unto the LORD for Israel**; and the LORD heard him. And as Samuel was offering up the burnt offering, the Philistines drew near to battle against Israel: but the LORD thundered with a great thunder on that day upon the Philistines, and discomfited them; and they were smitten before Israel."* (NKJV)

II. Fear – A Benefit or A Curse?

1 Sam. 7:7 – *"**they were afraid** of the Philistines."*

Luke 8:22-25 – *"One day Jesus got into a boat with his disciples and said to them, 'Let us go across to the other side of the lake.' So they started out. As they were sailing, Jesus fell asleep. Suddenly a strong wind blew down on the lake, and the boat began to fill with water, so that they were all in great danger. The disciples went to Jesus and woke him up, saying, 'Master, Master! We are about to die!'*

Jesus got up and gave an order to the wind and to the stormy water; they quieted down, and there was a great calm. Then he said to the disciples, 'Where is your faith?'

*But they were amazed and **afraid**, and said to one another, 'Who is this man? He gives orders to the winds and waves, and they obey him!'"* (TEV)

Whether a person was living under the Old covenant or presently living under the New Covenant, we all must learn to deal with the issue of fear.

There are **two kinds of fear** described in the Bible: Fear that can bring torment causing a person to cower behind closed doors and keep them from venturing out into the world; or fear that serves to motivate us to turn to the Lord for strength, so that we can boldly and confidently bear witness to the resurrection of Christ.

Ungodly fear as described in scripture:

1 John 4:18 – *"… Since fear is crippling, a fearful life—fear of death, fear of judgment—is one not yet fully formed in love."* (Msg)

Rev. 21:8 – *"But the cowardly, the unbelieving… their place will be in the fiery lake of burning sulfur. This is the second death."* (NIV)

1 Samuel 15:24 – *"Then Saul said to Samuel, 'I have sinned. I violated the Lord's command and your instructions. I was afraid of the people and so I gave in to them.'"* (NIV)

Godly fear as described in scripture:

Psalm 111:10 – *"The **fear** of the Lord is the beginning of wisdom…."* (NIV)

Deut. 10:12 – *"And now, O Israel, what does the Lord your God ask of you but to **fear** the Lord your God, to walk in all his ways, to love him, to serve the Lord your God with all your heart and with all your soul."* (NIV)

Job 4:6 – *"Doesn't your **fear** of God give you confidence and your lifetime of integrity give you hope?"* (GW)

Luke 12:4-5 – *"Dear friends, don't be afraid of those who want to kill you. They can only kill the body; they cannot do any more to you. But I'll tell you whom to fear. Fear God, who has the power to kill people and then throw them into hell."*

When you are afraid for your life and believe you are about to die, you will flee as the Israelites, "every man to his tent."

But, when you are willing to lose your life for Christ's sake and the gospel's, fear motivates you to call upon the Lord for strength enabling you to live in victory over the fear of death.

1 Cor. 15:55, **57** – *"'O death, where is your victory? O death, where is your sting?' How we thank God, who gives us victory over sin and death through Jesus Christ our Lord!"* (NLT)

Fleshly fear has torment and makes us wither, godly fear, the fear of the Lord, emboldens us to put our trust in Him and do His will.

III. Divine Intercession

1 Sam. 7:5, **8** – *"And Samuel said, Gather all Israel to Mizpeh, and **I will pray for you** unto the LORD. And the children of Israel said to Samuel, **Cease not** to cry unto the LORD our God for us, that he will save us out of the hand of the Philistines."* (NKJV)

1 Sam. 7:9 – *"And **Samuel** took a sucking lamb, and **offered** it for **a burnt offering** wholly unto the LORD: and **Samuel cried unto the LORD for Israel; and the LORD heard him**."* (NKJV)

Samuel, as a type of Christ, performs two ministries for Israel (the believer). The **first** is offering a lamb as the whole burnt offering, signifying total consecration and dedication of one's life to God; and the **second** is the ministry of intercessory prayer.

Eph. 5:1-2 – *"You are God's children whom he loves, so try to be like him. Live a life of love just as Christ loved us and gave himself for us as a sweet-smelling offering and sacrifice to God."* (NCV)

Galatians 2:20 – *"I am crucified with Christ: nevertheless I live; yet not I, but Christ liveth in me: and the life which I now live in the flesh I live by the faith of the Son of God, who loved me, and gave himself for me."* (KJV)

Choosing to be identified with Christ in His death, burial, and resurrection establishes the foundation for any believer to live the "crucified life." Dying to self and letting Christ live His life in and through you is the victorious Christian life.

The picture we gain in this text in Samuel is one of Christ offering Himself up to the Father as a sweet-smelling savor. He is doing that through the believer's life, by speaking His Word into the spiritual ear of the believer, which empowers the believer to be and do the will of God.

Rom. 10:17 – *"But it is in that way faith comes, from hearing, and that means hearing the word of Christ."* (NJB)

Hebrews 7:15-26 – *"The change in God's law is even more evident from the fact that a different priest, who is like Melchizedek, has now come. He became a priest, not by meeting the old requirement of belonging to the tribe of Levi, but by the power of a life that cannot be destroyed. And the psalmist pointed this out when he said of Christ, 'You are a priest forever in the line of Melchizedek.'*

Yes, the old requirement about the priesthood was set aside because it was weak and useless. For the law made nothing perfect, and now a better hope has taken its place. And that is how we draw near to God. God took an oath that Christ would always be a priest, but he never did this for any other priest. Only to Jesus did he say, 'The Lord has taken an oath and will not break his vow: You are a priest forever.' Because of God's oath, it is Jesus who guarantees the effectiveness of this better covenant.

*Another difference is that there were many priests under the old system. When one priest died, another had to take his place. But **Jesus** remains **a priest forever**; his priesthood will never end. Therefore **he is able**, once and forever, **to save everyone** who comes to God through him. He lives forever **to plead with God on their behalf.***

***He is the kind of high priest we need** because he is holy and blameless, unstained by sin. He has now been set apart from sinners, and he has been given the highest place of honor in heaven."* (NLT)

Jesus Christ **holds His priesthood permanently**. Jesus is the superior High Priest because He needs no successor. His priesthood is permanent. It is eternal!

The word **permanently** (*aparabatos*) means unchangeable, unalterable—something that *cannot* be changed. Jesus' priesthood does not just happen to be permanent. It is not capable of anything but permanence.

By its very divine nature it can never conclude or weaken or become ineffective. Jesus Christ has a priesthood that is absolutely incapable of ever being altered in any way! He is the last high priest. No other will ever be needed.

<u>**Heb. 7:25**</u> – *"Wherefore he is able also to save them **to the uttermost** those that come unto God by him, seeing he ever liveth to make intercession for them."* (KJV)

Jesus' priesthood is not only eternal and unalterable, but it is also unlimited in its scope. He saves **"to the uttermost"** (*panteles*); meaning completeness or perfection. The King James translation here is both accurate and significant.

The Old Testament sacrifices only symbolized the removal of sin. The symbol was God-given and God-required, but it still was only a temporary provision, a symbol of the permanent to come. However, Jesus Christ is able to save both eternally and completely.

Paul agreed with the Psalmist that God's "eternal power and divine nature" were evident for every person to see (<u>Psa. 19</u>)(<u>Rom. 1:18–20</u>). We call such evidence "general revelation", but it is definitely limited revelation.

The beauty of the animal kingdom and the majestic, clockwork dependability of the surging tides suggest God's creative abilities, wisdom, and power, but they don't communicate the necessary truth to bring man to a saving knowledge of God.

Both general revelation and the Old Testament sacrifices were given to us by God. But we can only learn about salvation from God's special revelation, from His written Word, the Bible.

When people say they can find God on the beach or in the wilderness or at the lake, it is a very superficial claim. While observing nature, we cannot possibly see clearly God's judgment on sin, the need for salvation, or "the way" to salvation. These are only seen with spiritual eyes, through the revelation of His Word.

"The nature of salvation is bringing men **near to God**. By delivering from sin, it qualifies believers to come to God. Deliverance from sin involves all three of the major tenses—past, present, and future."

In the **past tense**, we *have been* freed from sin's guilt (and punishment). In the **present tense**, we *are* freed from sin's power (<u>Rom. 6:14</u>) (<u>Rom. 8:2</u>). In the **future tense**, we *shall be* freed from sin's presence.

So every believer can say, "I have been saved" (in my spirit), "I am being saved" (in my soul), and "I shall be saved" (receiving a resurrection body, which is totally free from a sin nature). All these statements are true; all are scriptural. Together they represent the full, complete nature of our salvation." [11]

<u>Heb. 7:25</u> – *"He **always lives to make intercession** for us."*

The security of our salvation is Jesus' perpetual intercession for us. We can no more keep ourselves saved, than we can save ourselves in the first place. Jesus not only has power to save us, He has power to keep us. Jesus Christ will, constantly and perpetually, intercede for us before the Father.

So, do you want Jesus, the glorious High Priest of intercession in your corner, interceding on your behalf?

Do you want him sitting on the throne of your heart?

Do you want him offering up the daily sacrifice in your life?

Do you want him speaking His word of faith into your spirit, so you can be and do God's will?

Then you must give him his rightful place in your heart. You must make Him preeminent, putting Him before everything else.

---

[11]   MacArthur, J. 1996, c1983. *Hebrews 7:26*. Includes index. Moody Press: Chicago

Recognize Him as the true Judge, the one who will not only hold you accountable for all you say and do, but the one powerful enough to produce godly change in your life. He is the Savior!

Let the fear of the Lord give you confidence in your weakness, knowing that He is continually making intercession for you.

CHAPTER FOURTEEN

Understanding the Victorious Life of Christ

Gal. 2:20 – *"Christ's life showed me how, and enabled me to do it. I identified myself completely with him. Indeed, I have been crucified with Christ. My ego is no longer central. It is no longer important that I appear righteous before you or have your good opinion, and I am no longer driven to impress God. Christ lives in me. The life you see me living is not 'mine,' but it is lived by faith in the Son of God, who loved me and gave himself for me."* (LB)

Paul's confession to the Galatians helps us understand that living a victorious life as a Christian is really dependent upon our identification with Christ by picking up our cross daily and acknowledging that we have died to self so that Christ can live His life in and through us. When we don't identify with our new nature from Christ and lean on the Holy Spirit for wisdom and guidance, we end up relying on the arm of flesh and the result is our Adamic nature finds expression in our attitudes, speech, and actions.

This truth of death to self, by letting Christ live his life in and through us, is now depicted in our account in 1st Samuel. No longer is Eli (the flesh) offering up the sacrifices, now Samuel (Christ) is offering up the sacrifice in Israel (the believer).

1 Sam. 7:10-13 – *"And **as Samuel was offering** up the burnt offering, **the Philistines drew near to battle** against Israel. But the LORD thundered with a great thunder upon the Philistines that day, and so confused them that they were smitten before Israel. And the men of Israel went out of **Mizpah**, and pursued the Philistines, and drove them back as far as below **Bethcar**. Then Samuel took a stone, and set it up between Mizpah and Shen, and* *called its name **Ebenezer**, saying, 'Thus far the LORD has helped us.' So the Philistines were subdued, and they did not come anymore into the territory of Israel. And the hand of the LORD was against the Philistines **all the days of Samuel**."* (NKJV)

The Mizpah meeting, some eight miles north of Jerusalem, was one of the great revivals in Biblical history. Mizpah means "watchtower" and it was here that the Israelites gained a new perspective – concerning their own sin, concerning the Ark, and also in recognizing the authority of Samuel and allowing him to "judge" them.

In calling Israel to repentance and personal humbling, through fasting, Samuel was initiating a covenantal renewal. Along with the confession of their sins, they poured out the drink offering symbolizing their commitment and utter abandonment to God's purposes.

In addition, they gave Samuel his rightful place, as prophet, priest and judge. Samuel's offering of the whole burnt sacrifice symbolized the exercise of the Lordship and anointing of Jesus in Israel. They put away the false gods, and petitioned the prophetic intercession of Samuel. These are all vital parts of Israel's return to the Lord God.

In the same way, for you and I to experience this kind of spiritual renewal, we must demonstrate the same detailed returning to the Lord. We can't expect to experience Christ's victory in our lives if we leave out various aspects of this scenario.

I. Samuel Begins To Offer Up An Acceptable Sacrifice

Remember when God confronted Eli about the kind of sacrifice that was being offered in His sanctuary?

1 Sam. 2:29 – *"Why do you kick (rebel & scorn) at My sacrifice and at My offering which I have commanded in My dwelling, and honor your sons above Me, by making yourselves fat with the choicest of every offering of My people Israel?"* (NASB)

God has commanded "My sacrifice" and "My offering" to be offered in His dwelling place. What's God's New Testament dwelling place?

Eph. 2:20 – *"**We are his house**, built on the foundation of the apostles and the prophets. And the cornerstone is Christ Jesus himself."* (NLT)

Hebrews 3:6 – *"But Christ is faithful as a son over God's house. And we are his house, if we hold on to our courage and the hope of which we boast."* (NIV)

What kind of sacrifice does God want offered in His dwelling place? There is only one acceptable sacrifice that gives off a pleasing aroma to God.

Eph. 5:2 – *"Live a life filled with love, following the example of Christ. He loved us and offered himself as a sacrifice for us, a pleasing aroma to God."* (NLT)

It isn't the sacrifice or offering that we conclude is appropriate. It isn't our place to say, "I'll serve here and that will be enough" or "I'll give so much and that will be sufficient". We do not have the right to determine for ourselves what might be appropriate to offer to God.

No! Our heavenly Father has commanded a specific sacrifice and offering to be ascending from His dwelling place and that sacrifice and offering is none other than Christ, Himself.

That's why the apostle Paul says, "for to me to live is Christ" (Phil. 1:21).

Therefore, what makes us think that we can continue day after day without feeding on the Bread of Life, which is the Word of God, or live our lives, in victory over the sin nature, without being strengthened, through fresh communion with God through prayer and praise?

As New Testament believers, one of the questions we need to ask ourselves is: "As the dwelling place of God, what kind of offering is being offered up in my life?"

Are we continually offering up a **sin offering**, which acknowledges guilt arising from personal disobedience or are we offering up the **whole burnt offering**, which signifies the total commitment and complete dedication of our lives to God and His purposes?

Is the aroma ascending from our lives, the sweet smell of the increasing knowledge of Christ, or is it the sickening smell of our Adamic nature, expressing a self-centered, prideful, and independent attitude that is still conformed to a Godless world-system.

Romans 12:2 – *"Don't copy the behavior and customs of this world, but let God transform you into a new person by changing the way you think. Then you will know what God wants you to do, and you will know how good and pleasing and perfect his will really is."* (NLT)

How does God transform the way we think? Through faith – receiving Christ's living Word!

Rom. 10:17 – *"It is in that way faith comes, from hearing, and that means hearing the word of Christ."* (NJB)

Rom. 1:17 – *"For in the gospel a righteousness from God is revealed, a righteousness that is by faith from first to last, just as it is written: 'The righteous will live by faith.'"* (NIV)

Col. 3:16 – *"Let the words of Christ, in all their richness, live in your hearts and make you wise. Use **his** words to teach and counsel each other. Sing psalms and hymns and spiritual songs to God with thankful hearts."* (NLT)

Christ speaks His living Word into our spirit giving us faith from God and that Word confronts the wisdom of the world-system that has influenced our thinking. The truth contained in Scripture is made alive in our hearts and our mind is renewed as we meditate on it in His presence.

What kind of philosophies does the world-system promote in the 21st Century? You've heard of them: Darwinian-evolution; Rationalism; Existentialism; Secular Humanism; Post-modernism; Materialism; Reincarnation; Universalism; Pluralism; Situational ethics; Relativism; and many more.

However, as we listen and receive His Word into our hearts, we grow from faith to faith gaining in godly wisdom and the ability to teach and counsel each other. And the truth of Christ's Word confronts these false ideologies and sets us free to love God and do His will.

Coming to know Christ better allows for His life to be expressed through us in thought, word, and deed.

II. Christ Is The Faithful High Priest of Intercession

1 Sam. 7:10 – *"And as **Samuel** was offering up the burnt offering..."*

Another question we need to ask is, "From whom is the sacrifice originating?"

In chapter two, Eli asks the question: "Who will intercede for the sinner?" and leaves the question unanswered. However, here in chapter seven, Samuel answers that question by announcing: "I will intercede on your behalf."

Heb. 2:17 – *"Therefore, it was necessary for Jesus to be in every respect like us, his brothers and sisters, so that he could be our merciful and faithful High Priest before God. He then could offer a sacrifice that would take away the sins of the people."*

Heb. 4:14-15 – *"That is why we have a great High Priest who has gone to heaven, Jesus the Son of God. Let us cling to him and never stop trusting him. This High Priest of ours understands our weaknesses, for he faced all of the same temptations we do, yet he did not sin."*

Heb. 7:25 – *"It follows, then, that his power to save those who come to God through him is absolute, since he lives forever to intercede for them."* (NJB)

And the Holy Spirit dwelling within us, who knows our weaknesses and personal needs and the needs of our brothers and sisters in Christ, helps us pray according to the will of God, and in this way, we join with Jesus in His ministry of intercession.

Rom. 8:26 – *"And the Holy Spirit helps us in our distress. For we don't even know what we should pray for, nor how we should pray. But the Holy Spirit prays for us with groanings that cannot be expressed in words. And the Father who knows all hearts knows what the Spirit is saying, for the Spirit pleads for us believers in harmony with God's own will."*

III. Know That The Enemy Will Attack

1 Sam. 7:10 – *"the Philistines drew near to battle against Israel."*

The enemy of our soul doesn't want us to experience personal revival and if he thinks we are going to present a threat to the strongholds he has established in our lives, or in the community around us, he will draw near to do battle with us.

But fear not!

Rom. 8:31-39 – *"What can we say about such wonderful things as these? If God is for us, who can ever be against us? Since God did not spare even his own Son but gave him up for us all, won't God, who gave us Christ, also give us everything else? Who dares accuse us whom God has chosen for his own? Will God? No! He is the one who has given us right standing with himself. Who then will condemn us? Will Christ Jesus? No, for he is the one who died for us and was raised to life for us and is sitting at the place of highest honor next to God, pleading for us. Can anything ever separate us from Christ's love? Does it mean he no longer loves us if we have trouble or calamity, or are persecuted, or are hungry or cold or in danger or threatened with death?*

(Even the Scriptures say, 'For your sake we are killed every day; we are being slaughtered like sheep.') No, despite all these things, overwhelming victory is ours through Christ, who loved us. And I am convinced that nothing can ever separate us from his love. Death can't, and life can't. The angels can't, and the demons can't. Our fears for today, our worries about tomorrow, and even the powers of hell can't keep God's love away. Whether we are high above the sky or in the deepest ocean, nothing in all creation will ever be able to separate us from the love of God that is revealed in Christ Jesus our Lord."

IV. But God Thundered Against the Enemy – Israel is Victorious and Strongholds are Restored to Israel

Numerous passages in the King James Version of the New Testament begin by describing man's negative situation, and follow up with the phrase "but God", which presents hope in the midst of man's despair. For example:

Eph. 2:1-5 – *"And you He made alive, who were dead in trespasses and sins, in which you once walked according to the course of this world, according to the prince of the power of the air, the spirit who now works in the sons of disobedience, among whom also we all once conducted ourselves in the lusts of our flesh, fulfilling the desires of the flesh and of the mind, and were by nature children of wrath, just as the others.* **But God**, *who is rich in mercy, because of His great love with which He loved us, even when we were dead in trespasses, made us alive together with Christ (by grace you have been saved)."* (NKJV)

That phrase changes everything! Because all things are possible with God, nothing is impossible to the person who puts their trust in the Lord and believes His Word. "But God" makes all the difference in the world. The Philistines arrayed themselves for battle – **But God!**

Now, with their sins confessed and forgiven and with their lives consecrated and submitted to God, instead of using the Word of God as a fetish, they put their trust in God and the faithful intercession of Samuel, and God displayed His power and thundered against the enemy.

A terribly vicious storm struck the Philistines and they fled in terror from this divine visitation, and God's intervention allowed the men of Israel to drive the enemy off of their land as far as Bethcar.

God is the source of our victory. He has disarmed the enemy and now all we have to do is step forward in faith and drive the enemy from our borders.

You have real borders in your life – borders that God has given for you to rule over.

You are to rule over your human **spirit**, by submitting to the Holy Spirit and letting Him lead you into all truth.

You are to rule over your **soul** (thought life, decisions of the will, and emotional expressions) by not allowing the enemy to establish a stronghold in your soul.

God, also, instructs us to rule over our **body** and that means, "each of you should learn to control his own body in a way that is holy and honorable," ruling over our bodily appetites and "abstaining from sexual immorality" (1 Thess. 4:3-4) (Phil. 1:27).

Bethcar = "House or habitation of the Lamb". In other words, Bethcar was pastureland and part of God's provision for Israel.

One of the primary strategies of the enemy is to "invade and occupy." In order to keep us from enjoying all of God's provision, the enemy works to keep us from grazing in the pasture of God's Word, which is full of nutrients that will help us stay strong and healthy in the Lord.

The fact that "the hand of the Lord was against the Philistines all days of Samuel's life" stresses the need for the continued intercession of Samuel; and, as you and I submit to Christ's Lordship, we can count on His continuous intercession on our behalf.

V. The Necessity of A New Perspective

Why would Samuel call Israel to gather at Mizpah? Mizpah means "watchtower" and implies seeing from a more lofty perspective. A watchtower enables you to see the enemy coming and thus, make appropriate preparations. It also allows one to exchange their earthly view of life for a more heavenly one.

Col. 3:2-3 – *"Set your minds on things that are above, not on things that are on earth. For you have died, and your life is hidden with Christ in God."* (NLT)

Samuel set up a memorial and named the place **Ebenezer** (stone of help). That was the exact place of the earlier defeat by the Philistines. The Lord doesn't want us carrying around the memories of past defeats; rather He wants us to set up memorials to remember our victories through Him.

So, is defeat and suffering part of the path that brings us into triumph in Christ? Yes!

Hannah's personal struggle with barrenness motivated her to cry out in prayer to God and to ultimately reorder her priorities.

Initially, she was praying for her personal reproach to be lifted through childbearing. But, eventually, she touched the heart of God and began praying according to God's will and for God's need – a prophet and a faithful priest in the Land.

This in turn led to great blessings; she not only received a glorious vision of God, but was also blessed with a large family.

Israel's defeat and the **death of the men** who violated the sanctity of God's ark were definite tragedies. But the battle purged Eli's wicked sons from the priesthood; it brought Israel a new awareness of the holiness of God, and then it led to a spiritual revival. That revival made it possible for God to give Israel military victory and peace on its borders!

Rom. 8:28 – *"We are well aware that God works with those who love him, those who have been called in accordance with his purpose, and turns everything to their good."* (NLT)

In the end, Samuel, the man of prayer, was able to accomplish what Samson the man of strength could not accomplish for Israel.

The questions that all of us face today are: "What kind of sacrifice is being offered up in God's habitation? Is it what He has commanded or is it something we've concocted?

The apostle Paul addressed this question when writing to the Philippian believers. He said:

Phil. 3:4-8 – *"Yet I could have confidence in myself if anyone could. If others have reason for confidence in their own efforts, I have even more! For I was circumcised when I was eight days old, having been born into a pure-blooded Jewish family that is a branch of the tribe of Benjamin. So I am a real Jew if there ever was one! What's more, I was a member of the Pharisees, who demand the strictest obedience to the Jewish law. And zealous? Yes, in fact, I harshly persecuted the church. And I obeyed the Jewish law so carefully that I was never accused of any fault.*

I once thought all these things were so very important, but now I consider them worthless because of what Christ has done. Yes, everything else is worthless when compared with the priceless gain of knowing Christ Jesus my Lord. I have discarded everything else, counting it all as garbage, so that I may have Christ." (NLT)

Now, ask yourself: "Is the aroma arising from my life a sweet smelling savor?"

That can only be true if you are growing to know Christ better and are being conformed into His image.

Are you progressively learning to rule and reign in your spirit, soul, and body?

If the Holy Spirit is speaking to your heart and you feel convicted today about areas in your life that are still not surrendered to Christ? Then I want to encourage you to prayerfully repent.

God's Word instructs us to pray for one another.

James 5:16 – *"Confess your sins to each other and pray for each other so that you may be healed. The earnest prayer of a righteous person has great power and wonderful results."* (NLT)

VI. Samuel Judges Israel in Circuit Year by Year

1 Sam. 7:14-17 – *"Then the cities which the Philistines had taken from Israel were restored to Israel, from Ekron to Gath; and Israel recovered its territory from the hands of the Philistines. Also there was peace between Israel and the Amorites. And **Samuel judged Israel all the days of his life**. He went from year to year on a circuit to Bethel, Gilgal, and Mizpah, and judged Israel in all those places. But he always returned to Ramah, for his home was there. There he judged Israel, and there he built an altar to the Lord."* (NKJV)

It is God's will for each one of us to be conformed into the image of Christ. In order for that to happen experientially, God must take the initiative to be actively involved in our lives on a continual basis. The Lord does this by revisiting key growth points in our lives.

As long as we give Christ first place in our lives, and allow him to rule and motivate us, we can count on growing spiritually.

Let's look at these four key growth points as depicted by the cities Samuel visited in circuit.

A. Beth-el = means "house of God" and is mentioned more times in the Old Testament than any city except Jerusalem. It is the location where Abram first built an altar and began to worship the Lord.

Genesis 12:8 – *"After that, Abram traveled southward and set up camp in the hill country between Bethel on the west and Ai on the east. There he built an altar and worshiped the Lord."* (NLT)

Bethel was the place where Jacob received his vision of the angels of God ascending and descending on a heavenly ladder.

Gen. 28:11-22 – *"At sundown he arrived at a good place to set up camp and stopped there for the night. Jacob found a stone for a pillow and lay down to sleep. As he slept, he dreamed of a stairway that reached from earth to heaven. And he saw the angels of God going up and down on it. At the top of the stairway stood the Lord, and he said, 'I am the Lord, the God of your grandfather Abraham and the God of your father, Isaac. The ground you are lying on belongs to you. I will give it to you and your descendants. Your descendants will be as numerous as the dust of the earth! They will cover the land from east to west and from north to south. All the families of the earth will be blessed through you and your descendants. What's more, I will be with you, and I will protect you wherever you go. I will someday bring you safely back to this land. I will be with you constantly until I have finished giving you everything I have promised.'* (NLT)

Then Jacob woke up and said, 'Surely the Lord is in this place, and I wasn't even aware of it.' He was afraid and said, 'What an awesome place this is! It is none other than the house of God—the gateway to heaven!' The next morning he got up very early. He took the stone he had used as a pillow and set it upright as a memorial pillar. Then he poured olive oil over it. He named the place Bethel—'house of God'—though the name of the nearby village was Luz. (NLT)

Then Jacob made this vow: 'If God will be with me and protect me on this journey and give me food and clothing, and if he will bring me back safely to my father, then I will make the Lord my God. This memorial pillar will become a place for worshiping God, and I will give God a tenth of everything he gives me.'" (NLT)

Bethel was the place where Jacob encountered the Lord God on a personal level. Instead of simply giving mental ascent to the existence of the God of his father, Jacob was now converted to a personal faith in the Most High God. Here began his commitment to worship the Lord and acknowledge God's blessing in his life with the tithe of everything God enabled him to earn.

Bethel marks the beginning of our relationship with God and the time frame when God lays a foundation of truth in our lives. What we don't realize at the time of our infancy in Christ is that our foundation is inadequate to handle all the building that God wants to accomplish in us.

When addressing the Ephesian church in His revelation to the apostle John, Jesus confronted them regarding the cracks that had shown up in their foundation and had weakened their ability to express proper love for God and for each other. That's why God revisits the foundational truths in our lives to make sure we are still walking in the truth we originally embraced.

Rev. 2:4-5 – *"But I have this complaint against you. You don't love me or each other as you did at first! Look how far you have fallen from your first love! Turn back to me again and work as you did at first. If you don't, I will come and remove your lampstand from its place among the churches."* (NLT)

B. Gilgal = means "Liberty" or "rolling away". It is the place of the second circumcision.

Gilgal was Israel's first camping site once they had crossed the Jordan River. Here they erected the twelve stones taken from the bed of the Jordan River as a memorial to the fact that just as God had opened the Red Sea allowing their fathers to cross on dry land; God, also, dried up the waters of the Jordan allowing this new generation to cross-over on dry land.

Here, at Gilgal, they circumcised all the males born in the wilderness during Israel's 40 years of wandering. Here, they celebrated the first Passover in the land God had given to them. Also, here the wilderness provision of manna ceased.

Joshua 4:19-24 – *"The people crossed the Jordan on the tenth day of the first month—the month that marked their exodus from Egypt. They camped at Gilgal, east of Jericho. It was there at Gilgal that Joshua piled up the twelve* *stones taken from the Jordan River. Then Joshua said to the Israelites, 'In the future, your children will ask, 'What do these stones mean?' Then you can tell them, 'This is where the Israelites crossed the Jordan on dry ground.' For the Lord your God dried up the river right before your eyes, and he kept it dry until you were all across, just as he did at the Red Sea when he dried it up until we had all crossed over. He did this so that all the nations of the earth might know the power of the Lord, and that you might fear the Lord your God forever."*

Joshua 5:2-12 – *"At that time the Lord told Joshua, 'Use knives of flint to make the Israelites a circumcised people again.' So Joshua made flint knives and circumcised the entire male population of Israel at Gibeath-haaraloth.* (NLT)

Joshua had to circumcise them because all the men who were old enough to bear arms when they left Egypt had died in the wilderness. Those who left Egypt had all been circumcised, but none of those born after the Exodus, during the years in the wilderness, had been circumcised. The Israelites wandered in the wilderness for forty years until all the men who were old enough to bear arms when they left Egypt had died. For they had disobeyed the Lord, and the Lord vowed he would not let them enter the land he had sworn to give us—a land flowing with milk and honey. So Joshua circumcised their sons who had not been circumcised on the way to the Promised Land—those who had grown up to take their fathers' places. After all the males had been circumcised, they rested in the camp until they were healed.

Then the Lord said to Joshua, 'Today I have rolled away the shame of your slavery in Egypt.' So that place has been called Gilgal to this day.

While the Israelites were camped at Gilgal on the plains of Jericho, they celebrated Passover on the evening of the fourteenth day of the first month—the month that marked their exodus from Egypt. The very next day they began to eat unleavened bread and roasted grain harvested from the land. No manna appeared that day, and it was never seen again. So from that time on the Israelites ate from the crops of Canaan."

Concerning physical circumcision, the scripture is clear. Abraham received the sign of circumcision as a seal to confirm that he had already believed in the Word of God and that God had accepted him and declared him to be righteous. Note that circumcision followed the exercise of Abraham's faith in God.

Romans 4:9-10 – *"Now then, is this blessing only for the Jews, or is it for Gentiles, too? Well, what about Abraham? We have been saying he was declared righteous by God because of his faith. But how did his faith help him? Was he declared righteous only after he had been circumcised, or was it before he was circumcised? The answer is that God accepted him first, and then he was circumcised later!"* (NLT)

But Gilgal speaks of a second circumcision, to what is this second circumcision referring?

Eph. 2:11 – *"Don't forget that you Gentiles used to be outsiders by birth. You were called "the uncircumcised ones" by the Jews, who were proud of their circumcision, even though it affected only their bodies and not their hearts."* (NLT)

Gal. 6:15 – *"It doesn't make any difference now whether we have been circumcised or not. What counts is whether we really have been changed into new and different people."* (NLT)

Phil. 3:2-3 – *"Watch out for those dogs, those wicked men and their evil deeds, those mutilators who say you must be circumcised to be saved. For we who worship God in the Spirit are the only ones who are truly circumcised. We put no confidence in human effort. Instead, we boast about what Christ Jesus has done for us."* (NLT)

Col. 2:11 – *"When you came to Christ, you were 'circumcised,' but not by a physical procedure. It was a spiritual procedure—the cutting away of your sinful nature."* (NLT)

Gilgal represents the 'cutting away of your sin nature.' It represents the truth of 'picking up your cross daily and reckoning upon the fact that when Christ died, you died with Christ to the sin nature.

Romans 6:6-13 – *"Our old sinful selves were crucified with Christ so that **sin** (the rebellious nature) might lose its power in our lives. We are no longer slaves to sin. For when we died with Christ we were set free from the power of sin. And since we died with Christ, we know we will also share his new life. We are sure of this because Christ rose from the dead, and he will never die again. Death no longer has any power over him. He died once to defeat sin, and now he lives for the glory of God. So you should consider yourselves dead to sin and able to live for the glory of God through Christ Jesus.*

Do not let sin control the way you live; do not give in to its lustful desires. Do not let any part of your body become a tool of wickedness, to be used for sinning. Instead, give yourselves completely to God since you have been given new life. And use your whole body as a tool to do what is right for the glory of God." (NLT)

2 Cor. 4:11-12 – *"For we who live are constantly being delivered over to death for Jesus' sake, that **the life of Jesus** also may be manifested in our mortal flesh. So death works in us, but life in you."* (NASB)

Our ability to demonstrate the life of Christ and minister his life to others is directly related to the exercise of our faith in putting off the manifestations of our sin nature and actively yielding our members as instruments of righteousness to God. This we must do in very practical ways.

Col. 3:1-10 – *"Since you have been raised to new life with Christ, set your sights on the realities of heaven, where Christ sits at God's right hand in the place of honor and power. Let heaven fill your thoughts. Do not think only about things down here on earth. For you died when Christ died, and your real life is hidden with Christ in God. And when Christ, who is your real life, is revealed to the whole world, you will share in all his glory.*

So put to death the sinful, earthly things lurking within you. Have nothing to do with sexual sin, impurity, lust, and shameful desires. Don't be greedy for the good things of this life, for that is idolatry. God's terrible anger will come upon those who do such things. You used to do them when your life was still part of this world. But now is the time to get rid of anger, rage, malicious behavior, slander, and dirty language. Don't lie to each other, for you have stripped off your old evil nature and all its wicked deeds. In its place you have clothed yourselves with a brand-new nature that is continually being renewed as you learn more and more about Christ, who created this new nature within you." (NLT)

C. Mizpah = means "watch-tower" or "exalted viewpoint".

Mizpah represents the transformation God wants to take place in our lives when we begin to experience a new mindset. That's why God raised us up and seated us in heavenly places with Christ, so we could begin to understand life from a different perspective. (Eph. 2:5-7)

Rom. 12:2 – *"Don't be like the people of this world, but let God change the way you think. Then you will know how to do everything that is good and pleasing to him."* (CEV)

I recently watched a tremendous Biblical Worldview teaching entitled, "The Truth Project", produced by *Focus on the Family*. I believe that all who watch that DVD series should begin to realize the importance and necessity of changing the way we think to conform to God's perspective.

Barna Research released the results of a 2002 -2003 survey, which sought to identify how many people in America possessed a "Biblical Worldview." The article was entitled: ***A Biblical Worldview Has a Radical Effect on a Person's Life.***

A new research study from the Barna Research Group suggests that a large share of the nation's moral and spiritual challenges is directly attributable to the absence of a biblical worldview among Americans.

Citing the findings from a just-completed national survey of 2033 adults that showed only 4% of adults have a biblical worldview as the basis of their decision-making, researcher George Barna described the outcome. "If Jesus Christ came to this planet as a model of how we ought to live, then our goal should be to act like Jesus. Sadly, few people consistently demonstrate the love, obedience and priorities of Jesus. The primary reason that people do not act like Jesus is because they do not think like Jesus. Behavior stems from what we think - our attitudes, beliefs, values and opinions. Although most people own a Bible and know some of its content, our research found that most Americans have little idea how to integrate core biblical principles to form a unified and meaningful response to the challenges and opportunities of life. We're often more concerned with survival amidst chaos than with experiencing truth and significance."

The research indicated that everyone has a worldview, but relatively few people have a biblical worldview - even among devoutly religious people. The survey discovered that only 9% of born again Christians have such a perspective on life. The numbers were even lower among other religious classifications: Protestants (7%), adults who attend mainline Protestant churches (2%) and Catholics (less than one-half of 1%). The denominations that produced the highest proportions of adults with a biblical worldview were non-denominational Protestant churches (13%), Pentecostal churches (10%) and Baptist churches (8%).

Among the most prevalent alternative worldviews was postmodernism, which seemed to be the dominant perspective among the two youngest generations (i.e., the Busters and Mosaics).

For the purposes of the research, a biblical worldview was defined as believing that absolute moral truths exist; that such truth is defined by the Bible; and firm belief in six specific religious views. Those views were that Jesus Christ lived a sinless life; God is the all-powerful and all knowing Creator of the universe and He stills rules it today; salvation is a gift from God and cannot be earned; Satan is real; a Christian has a responsibility to share their faith in Christ with other people; and the Bible is accurate in all of its teachings."

Mizpah speaks of a Christ initiated reformation in the believer. It was at Mizpah that the nation of Israel gathered under the leadership of Samuel and then repented in deep humiliation on account of their sins. There they renewed their commitment to obey the Lord and acknowledged their covenant relationship with the God of their fathers.

It was at Mizpah that the Israelites put away the false gods of the nations around them. At Mizpah, they put away the pleasure-seeking immorality of the nearby cultures.

D. Ramah = means "heavenlies" or "abiding presence".

Not only did the Father give us seating with Christ in the heavenlies so that we would gain a divine perspective on life, but He gave us this seating so that we would learn to reign with Christ out of an intimate union with the heart of God.

Eph. 2:6-7 – *"In our **union with Christ Jesus** he raised us up with him **to rule with him** in the heavenly world. He did this to demonstrate for all time to come the extraordinary greatness of his grace in the love he showed us in Christ Jesus."* (TEV)

The foundation of our spiritual relationship with God is established through our new birth experience when we place our faith in Jesus Christ. This is typified by the city of **Bethel**.

As we grow in Christ, we receive a revelation of our need to experience the circumcision of our hearts, which is typified by the city of **Gilgal**.

As we continue to grow up into Christ our head, we receive a revelation of our need to gain the mind of Christ, which is a Biblical Worldview. We gain this new perspective through crying out to God for personal revival, surrender to the Lordship of Christ, and the dedication of our lives to His purposes in the earth.

This revelation of the Holy Spirit that we are raised up and seated with Christ in the heavenly realms is typified by the city of **Mizpah**.

Then, learning to rule and reign with Christ in the here and now means we must grow in our understanding of the Kingdom of Heaven. Through our being properly related to the government of the Kingdom of Heaven and understanding the delegated authority given to us by Jesus, as His ambassadors, we are to bring the blessings of the Kingdom of Heaven to earth.

Matt. 10:1 – *"And he called to him his twelve disciples and gave them authority over unclean spirits, to cast them out, and to heal every disease and every affliction."* (ESV)

Matt. 10:7-8 – *"Go and announce to them that the Kingdom of Heaven is near. Heal the sick, raise the dead, cure those with leprosy, and cast out demons. Give as freely as you have received!"* (NLT)

John 14:12 – *"Truly, truly, I say to you, whoever believes in me will also do the works that I do; and greater works than these will he do, because I am going to the Father."* (ESV)

John 20:21 – *"Again Jesus said, "Peace be with you! As the Father has sent me, I am sending you."* (NIV)

Matt. 28:18-20 – *"Jesus came and told his disciples, 'I have been given complete authority in heaven and on earth. Therefore, go and make disciples of all the nations, baptizing them in the name of the Father and the Son and the Holy Spirit. Teach these new disciples to obey all the commands I have given you. And be sure of this: I am with you always, even to the end of the age.'"* (NLT)

On the basis of Jesus Christ's authority and our union with Him, we are to go and **do** the works of Jesus and **proclaim** the good news of His saving grace and power.

Acts 1:1-3 – *"Dear Theophilus: In my first book I told you about everything Jesus began to **do** and **teach** until the day he ascended to heaven after giving his chosen apostles further instructions from the Holy Spirit. During the forty days after his crucifixion, he appeared to the apostles from time to time and proved to them in many ways that he was actually alive. On these occasions he talked to them about the Kingdom of God."* (NLT)

The book of Acts is the account of the disciples of Jesus continuing to do and teach what He began. This we also are to continue doing until He comes again. However, in order to obey His commands, we must be delivered from the domination of our sin nature and learn to live by His victorious life.

God will use calamity and loss to set you free from trusting in your flesh. Stay free, so you are free to do His will.

Galatians 5:1, 13 – "Christ has freed us so that we may enjoy the benefits of freedom. Therefore, be firm {in this freedom}, and don't become slaves again. You were indeed called to be free, brothers and sisters. Don't turn this freedom into an excuse for your corrupt nature to express itself. Rather, serve each other through love." (GW)

May His grace truly prevail in every way in your life and may Jesus be glorified in you.

ABBREVIATIONS:

KJV = *The Holy Bible : King James Version*. electronic ed. of the 1769 edition of the 1611 Authorized Version. Bellingham WA: Logos Research Systems, Inc., 1995

NKJV = *The New King James Version*. Nashville: Thomas Nelson, 1982

NIV = *The Holy Bible : New International Version*. electronic ed. Grand Rapids : Zondervan, 1996, c1984 "Scripture taken from HOLY BIBLE, NEW INTERNATIONAL VERSION®. Copyright © 1973, 1978, 1984 by International Bible Society. Used by permission of Zondervan Publishing House."

NLT = Tyndale House Publishers: *Holy Bible: New Living Translation*. 2nd ed. Wheaton, Ill.: Tyndale House Publishers, 2004

ESV = *The Holy Bible : English Standard Version*. Wheaton: Standard Bible Society, 2001 "Scripture quotations are from The Holy Bible, English Standard Version®, copyright © 2001 by Crossway Bibles, a publishing ministry of Good News Publishers. Used by permission. All rights reserved."

NCV = *The Everyday Bible: New Century Version*. Nashville, TN. : Thomas Nelson, Inc., 2005 "Scriptures quoted from *The Holy Bible: New Century Version*®, copyright © 2005 by Thomas Nelson, Inc. Used by permission."